THE FORMS OF ACTION

THE FORMS OF ACTION
AT COMMON LAW

A COURSE OF LECTURES

BY

F. W. MAITLAND

EDITED BY A.H.CHAYTOR AND
W.J.WHITTAKER

CAMBRIDGE UNIVERSITY PRESS

CAMBRIDGE
LONDON · NEW YORK · MELBOURNE

Published by the Syndics of the Cambridge University Press
The Pitt Building, Trumpington Street, Cambridge CB2 IRP
Bentley House, 200 Euston Road, London NW1 2DB
32 East 57th Street, New York, NY 10022, USA
296 Beaconsfield Parade, Middle Park, Melbourne 3206, Australia

ISBN 0 521 05657 8 hard covers
ISBN 0 521 09185 3 paperback

First published (with *Equity*) 1909
Reprinted 1910 1913 1916
1920 1926 1929 1932
First published seperately 1936
Reprinted 1941 1948 (twice) 1954
1958 1962 1963 1965
Reset and reprinted 1969
Reprinted 1971 1976

Printed in Great Britain
at the
University Printing House, Cambridge
(Euan Phillips, University Printer)

PUBLISHERS' NOTE

These lectures were first published in 1909, three years after Maitland's death. They were included in a volume entitled *Equity*, with a course of lectures on the latter subject. The following is the relevant extract from the editors' preface to the volume:

'To the twenty-one lectures on Equity we have added seven lectures upon the Forms of Action at Common Law, in order to present at the same time Maitland's account of the development of the two systems which grew up side by side. Here was the structure upon which rested the whole common law of England, and, as Maitland says, "the forms of action we have buried but they still rule us from their graves." The evasion of the burden of archaic procedure and of such barbaric tests of truth as battle, ordeal and wager of law, by the development of new forms and new law out of criminal or quasi criminal procedure and the inquest of neighbour-witnesses has never been described with this truth and clearness. He makes plain a great chapter of legal history which the learners and even the lawyers of today have almost abandoned in despair. The text of the chief writs is given after the lectures . . .

'In the editing of these latter lectures Mr E. T. Sandars, of the Inner Temple, also one of Maitland's pupils, has given us much invaluable help.'

After the lapse of more than a quarter of a century there is still a demand for the lectures on Equity, but the developments of that period have necessitated considerable annotation. This fact makes it desirable that the two courses shall be published separately, and the lectures on Forms of Action are therefore now being made available to students in a separate inexpensive volume. No annotation has been undertaken, the only change that has been made is to print the Table of Contents before instead of after the text.

1936

CONTENTS

LECTURE III

Sketch of the order in which forms of action developed. Periods: (I) 1066–1154. Litigation still mainly in local courts. King's court has (1) pleas of the crown, (2) suits between tenants in capite, (3) complaints of default of justice in lower courts (16, 17).

(II) 1154–89. Reign of Henry II, Glanvill's book. Writs assumed distinct forms, each begins a particular form of action (17).

1. The Writ of Right. Henry ordained that no man need answer for his freehold without royal writ (17). A man disseised of his freehold unjustly and without judgment has action in the king's court (17). This means that all litigation about freeholds in the local courts must begin by the king's writ (18, 19).

Breve de recto tenendo orders a lord to do justice (18).

Praecipe quod reddat or *praecipe in capite* used where the king's court had jurisdiction (18). Term 'Writ of Right' comes to include both forms (19). Action by Writ of Right slow and dilatory (19). Essoins (20). Trial by battle or the 'Grand Assize', i.e. twelve knights (21).

2. The Three Possessory Actions, traceable to Roman interdict (22).

(*a*) **The Assize of Novel Disseisin** (22, 23).

(*b*) **The Assize of Mort d'Ancestor** (23). Where a man has died seised as of fee his heir will be put into seisin. Action limited to 'the degrees' (25). This defect remedied by supplementary actions of **Aiel, Besaiel** and **Cosinage** with more modern procedure (25).

(*c*) **The Assize of Darrein Presentment.** Principle, that he who last presented to a benefice or his heir should do so again (25, 26).

A fourth assize: (*d*) **The Assize Utrum** to decide whether land was lay fee or ecclesiastical (26, 27). Later this action changed into 'the parson's writ of right' (27).

Certain questions begin to be tried by '*jurata*' (28). Recognitions (28). Differences between a 'jurata' and an 'assisa' (28).

Dower: two actions, the **Writ of Right of Dower** bidding the lord do justice in his court, and the **Writ of Dower unde nihil habet** brought in the king's court (29, 30). A third action, the writ of **Admeasurement of Dower** (30).

Action to recover a serf by writ **de nativo habendo.** Writ **de libertate probanda** given to alleged serf calling on the would be lord to prove his case in the king's court (30).

Personal actions in Glanvill's day are mostly in local courts (31).

Debt or **detinue of chattels,** writ similar to *Praecipe in capite,* little distinction between 'I own' and 'I am owed'. No jury or grand assize (31).

Gages of land made usually by demise of a term. This gave rise to several writs. Writ for gagee calling gagor to pay; and writ for gagor calling on gagee to take his money and return the land. This latter (form given) is a *Praecipe* for land with a reason and is the forerunner of the writs of Entry (31, 32). If the tenant says he holds in fee either party can have a 'recognition' to decide the question 'fee or gage'. But otherwise battle or the grand assize will decide the main question (32). Certain rules as to sealed charters exist but means of proof are not explained (32).

LECTURE IV

(III) 1189–1272. Third Period. Ric., Joh. and Hen. III. Rapid growth of writs *de cursu.* Registers formed (33). Between proprietary and possessory actions there grow up **Writs of Entry** alleging some particular flaw in the tenant's title; very numerous; originally limited by the 'degrees'; restriction abolished by Stat. of Marlborough 1267, creating writs in the *post* (33).

Confusion of English real actions due to these writs (34). Until death of Henry II all is simple. The proprietary and possessory actions are distinct. Then come Writs of Entry, extended by 1267 to every flaw in title. They are possessory in origin but proprietary in working (35). Blackstone thought them older than the assizes (36).

Other gaps are filled, writs of **Aiel, Besaiel** and **Cosinage,** also new writs relating to advowsons, wardships and marriages, easements, common rights and nuisance, frequently two forms—one regarded as proprietary the other as possessory (37).

Remedies of termors under the new writs. At first termor's sole remedy by **Covenant:** recovers the land but only against lessor (37, 38). About 1237 writ **Quare ejecit infra terminum,** invented by Raleigh. It gives termor a protected 'possession', subsequently distinguished from 'seisin'. But it is held to lie only against persons claiming under the lessor (38).

Personal actions make their appearance. **Debt-Detinue,** differentiated in the 13th century. In Detinue there is no specific restitution, hence Bracton says there is no real action for chattels (38).

Replevin for chattels distrained: invented *temp.* John (39).

Covenant, early 13th century, restricted to the recovery of terms of years and sealed writing required (39).

Account, appears *temp.* Henry III, a rare action and only against bailiffs (39).

Trespass. This is the most important. Instances *temp.* John, but it became a writ of course, late *temp.* Henry III. It originates in criminal law (the appeal of felony) (39). The defendant if found guilty is fined and imprisoned, not merely amerced. If he will not appear he can be seized or outlawed (40). At first real 'force and arms' probably necessary but later the least wrongful force is held to be enough (40).

Trial by jury is becoming normal trial for disputed facts and is slowly superseding the older forms, but compurgation survives in Debt and Detinue (40).

(IV) 1272–1307. Fourth Period. The reign of Edward I (41). Period of Statutory activity. Stat De Donis gives **Formedon in the Descender.** Writs *in consimili casu.* The tale of non-statutory actions complete. The king's courts have come to be omnicompetent, working all civil justice through these forms of action (41, 42).

LECTURE V

(V) 1307–1833. A long period but difficult to break up. Chief interest lies in development of **Trespass** (43).

Trespass *vi et armis* common from Edw. I's day. Main varieties (1) assault and battery, (2) *de bonis asportatis* and (3) *quare clausum fregit*. Unlawful force essential (43). Trespass can protect possession of land (43). **Trespass quare clausum fregit.** This writ given to the termor in 15th century (43); 'possession and seisin' (45). Tenant in Villeinage gets protection; by end of 15th century even against his lord (45). At end of 14th century action merely gave damages. *Temp.* Hen. VII the land itself can be recovered (45). *Quare ejecit infra terminum* not to be confused with Trespass *de ejectione firmae* (46). Latter becomes **Ejectment** and is extended by fiction to all claimants of land (46). Reasons for this (46). Description of the fiction of Ejectment (47, 48). During Tudor reigns Ejectment supplants the real actions (48). In some cases, e.g. where entry 'tolled', Ejectment not available (48). Ejectment was remodelled by C.L.P. Act, 1852, and was in use until 1875 (49).

Personal Actions (49).

Replevin, action for wrongful distraint (50).

Detinue, damages always alternative to return of goods. Hence chattels not 'real' property (50, 51). Ancient and modern views as to property in chattels (51). Wager of law (51).

Debt, originally purely recuperatory, later used to enforce all contracts for a fixed sum of money, and all fixed sums due (51, 52). But Debt admits of wager of law (52).

Account, originally for bailiffs only, superseded by Chancery Bill for account (52).

Covenant. Lessee's only remedy at one time; he recovers the land itself by the action of covenant real. In 13th century the seal becomes a necessity for covenant (52).

LECTURE VI

Trespass, appears about 1250. *Vi et armis contra pacem* (53). Trespass is to (1) land, (2) body, (3) chattels (53). Vanquished defendant *in misericordia* and liable to *capias pro fine* (53). Statute of Westminster II, writs *in consimili casu* result in the extension of trespass (53, 54).

Trespass upon the Special Case or **Case,** where the words *contra pacem* are left out. Falls apart during 15th century (54). Slander and Libel and Negligence and Deceit grow up within Case which becomes a sort of residuary action (54). *Capias pro fine* abolished (55). Distinction between Case and Trespass (55).

Assumpsit an offshoot of Case (55), involved the ideas of misfeasance and deceit (55, 56). Earliest are cases of misfeasance, then of negligence by bailees, then of breaches of warranty, then of non-feasance and Assumpsit becomes a separate action (beginning of 16th century) (56). Assumpsit then begins to do the work of Debt. **Indebitatus Assumpsit** (56, 57). This extended to implied contract and quasi-contract (57).

Trover (57): another branch of Case. Comes into existence about the middle of 16th century. Action supplanted Detinue (58). Since C.L.P. Act, 1854, courts have had power to order specific restitution of the chattel. Old option of paying the value no longer a right of the defendant (58). Thus Trespass and its offspring, Ejectment, Assumpsit, Trover and Case are substantially the only actions in common use (58). Replevin still used against a distrainor (58). Account and Dower practically superseded by Chancery remedies.

LECTURE VII

Attempts to classify Actions. Justinian's classifications (59). Do not well fit the English Actions. Bracton lays down that there is no action *in rem* for moveable goods because the possessor has the option of paying damages instead of giving up the thing. From this distinction come the terms 'Real' and 'Personal' property (60). Hence the extension of idea of Tort in England far beyond the Roman *maleficium* because it is conceived that all 'personal' actions must be founded either on contract or tort (60). Mere possession by the wrong person however honest is held a tort (61). Distribution of all actions between Contract and Tort never very easy or very successful (61). Position of Detinue (61). Mesne process is used by Bracton as the test of a real or personal action (61, 62). In later times however the final result attained becomes the test (62). Position of Ejectment and Covenant Real (62). The Action for mesne profits originated in this idea of mere possession, however honest, being a tort done to the true owner (63).

Past importance of procedure (63). The great textbooks were treatises on procedure. Formal decay set in soon after Edward I but a great development of substantive law was brought about by fictions (63, 64). This is a long process with two stages. (1) The stage of evasory fiction. Trespass usurps the work of other actions. Again steps in procedure are omitted or are feigned (64). Even the original writ was omitted unless the record had to be made up (64). Capture of Common Pleas jurisdiction by King's Bench and Exchequer (64). The King's Bench fiction, all actions begun by an action of Trespass and the arrest of the defendant: the Exchequer fiction—the *quo minus* (64). The reason for this stealing of business; partly due to the monopoly of Serjeants-at-law in the Common Pleas (64, 65). The Order of the Coif (64).

(2) End of the forms of action:

The Unification of Process Act, 1832 (65).

3 and 4 Will. IV, c. 27, sec. 36 abolishing Real and Mixed Actions (65).

3 and 4 Will. IV, c. 42 abolishing wager of law (65).

The Common Law Procedure Act, 1852. No form of action was thenceforward to be mentioned in the writ (65).

The Judicature Acts. Forms of action are finally abolished (65), this results in greater clearness of exposition, greater attention to the real substance of the law itself (66).

SELECT WRITS

Beginning with those relating to land (67).

LECTURE I

I propose to begin by speaking briefly of the Forms of Action, with especial relation to those which protected the possession and ownership of land. It may—I am well aware of it—be objected that procedure is not a good theme for academic discussion. Substantive law should come first—adjective law, procedural law, afterwards. The former may perhaps be studied in a university, the latter must be studied in chambers. As to obsolete procedure, a knowledge of it can be profitable to no man, least of all to a beginner. With this opinion I cannot agree. Some time ago I wished to say a little about seisin, which still, with all our modern improvements, is one of the central ideas of Real Property Law; but to say that little I found impossible if I could not assume some knowledge of the forms of action. Let us remember one of Maine's most striking phrases, 'So great is the ascendancy of the Law of Actions in the infancy of Courts of Justice, that substantive law has at first the look of being gradually secreted in the interstices of procedure.'[1] Assuredly this is true of our real property law, it has been secreted in the interstices of the forms of action. The system of Forms of Action or the Writ System is the most important characteristic of English medieval law, and it was not abolished until its piecemeal destruction in the nineteenth century.[2]

What was a form of action? Already owing to modern reforms it is impossible to assume that every law student must have heard or read or discovered for himself an answer to that question, but it is still one which must be answered if he is to have more than a very superficial knowledge of our law as it stands even at the present day. The forms of action we have buried, but they still rule us from their graves. Let us then for awhile place ourselves in Blackstone's day, or, for this matters not, some seventy years later in 1830, and let us look for a moment at English civil procedure.

Let it be granted that one man has been wronged by another; the first thing that he or his advisers have to consider is what form of action he shall bring. It is not enough that in some way or another he should compel his adversary to appear in court and should then state in the words that naturally occur to him the facts on which he relies and the remedy to which he thinks himself entitled. No, English law knows a certain number of forms of action, each with its own uncouth name, a

[1] Maine, *Early Law and Custom*, p. 389. [2] See below, p. 6.

writ of right, an assize of novel disseisin or of *mort d'ancestor*, a writ of entry *sur disseisin* in the *per* and *cui*, a writ of *besaiel*, of *quare impedit*, an action of covenant, debt, detinue, replevin, trespass, assumpsit, ejectment, case. This choice is not merely a choice between a number of queer technical terms, it is a choice between methods of procedure adapted to cases of different kinds. Let us notice some of the many points that are implied in it.

(i) There is the competence of the court. For very many of the ordinary civil cases each of the three courts which have grown out of the king's court of early days, the King's Bench, Common Pleas and Exchequer is equally competent, though it is only by means of elaborate and curious fictions that the King's Bench and the Exchequer can entertain these matters, and the Common Pleas still retains a monopoly of those actions which are known as real.

(ii) A court chosen, one must make one's adversary appear; but what is the first step towards this end? In some actions one ought to begin by having him summoned, in others one can at once have him attached, he can be compelled to find gage and pledge for his appearance. In the assize of novel disseisin it is enough to attach his bailiff.

(iii) Suppose him contumacious, what can one do? Can one have his body seized? If he cannot be found, can one have him outlawed? This stringent procedure has been extending itself from one form of action to another. Again, can one have the thing in dispute seized? This is possible in some actions, impossible in others.

(iv) Can one obtain a judgment by default, obtain what one wants though the adversary continues in his contumacy? Yes in some forms, no in others.

(v) It comes to pleading, and here each form of action has some rules of its own. For instance the person attacked—the tenant he is called in some cases, the defendant in others—wishes to oppose the attacker—the demandant he is called in some actions, the plaintiff in others—by a mere general denial, casting upon him the burden of proving his own case, what is he to say? In other words, what is the general issue appropriate to this action? In one form it is *Nihil debet*, in another *Non assumpsit*, in another 'Not guilty', in others, *Nul tort, nul disseisin*.

(vi) There is to be a trial; but what mode of trial? Very generally of course a trial by jury. But it may be trial by a grand or petty assize, which is not quite the same thing as trial by jury; or in Blackstone's day it may still conceivably be a trial by battle. Again in some forms of action the defendant may betake himself to the world-old process of compurgation or wager of law. Again there are a few issues which are tried without a jury by the judges who hear witnesses.

(vii) Judgment goes against the defendant, what is the appropriate form of execution? Can one be put into possession of the thing that has been in dispute? Can one imprison the defendant? Can one have him made an outlaw? or can he merely be distrained?

(viii) Judgment goes against the defendant. It is not enough that he should satisfy the plaintiff's just demand; he must also be punished for his breach of the law—such at all events is the theory. What form shall this punishment take? Will an amercement suffice, or shall there be fine or imprisonment? Here also there have been differences.

(ix) Some actions are much more dilatory than others; the dilatory ones have gone out of use, but still they exist. In these oldest forms— forms invented when as yet the parties had to appear in person and could only appoint attorneys by the king's special leave—the action may drag on for years, for the parties enjoy a power of sending essoins, that is, excuses for non-appearance. The medieval law of essoins is vast in bulk; time is allowed for almost every kind of excuse for non-appearance —a short essoin *de malo veniendi*, a long essoin *de malo lecti*. Nowadays all is regulated by general rules with a wide discretion left in the Court. In the Middle Ages discretion is entirely excluded; all is to be fixed by iron rules. This question of essoins has been very important—in some forms, the oldest and solemnest, a party may betake himself to his bed and remain there for year and day and meanwhile the action is suspended.

These remarks may be enough to show that the differences between the several forms of action have been of very great practical importance —'a form of action' has implied a particular original process, a particular mesne process, a particular final process, a particular mode of pleading, of trial, of judgment. But further to a very considerable degree the substantive law administered in a given form of action has grown up independently of the law administered in other forms. Each procedural pigeon-hole contains its own rules of substantive law, and it is with great caution that we may argue from what is found in one to what will probably be found in another; each has its own precedents. It is quite possible that a litigant will find that his case will fit some two or three of these pigeon-holes. If that be so he will have a choice, which will often be a choice between the old, cumbrous, costly, on the one hand, the modern, rapid, cheap, on the other. Or again he may make a bad choice, fail in his action, and take such comfort as he can from the hints of the judges that another form of action might have been more successful. The plaintiff's choice is irrevocable; he must play the rules of the game that he has chosen. Lastly he may find that, plausible as his case may seem, it just will not fit any one of the receptacles provided by the courts and he may take to himself the lesson that where there is no remedy there is no wrong.

The keynote of the form of action is struck by the original writ, the writ whereby the action is begun. From of old the rule has been that no one can bring an action in the king's courts of common law without the king's writ; we find this rule in Bracton—*Non potest quis sine brevi agere.*[1] That rule we may indeed say has not been abolished even in our own day. The first step which a plaintiff has to take when he brings an action in the High Court of Justice is to obtain a writ. But there has been a very great change. The modern writ is in form a command by the king addressed to the defendant telling him no more than that within eight days he is to appear, or rather to cause an appearance to be entered for him, in an action at the suit of the plaintiff, and telling him that in default of his so doing the plaintiff may proceed in his action and obtain a judgment. Then on the back of this writ the plaintiff, in his own or his adviser's words, states briefly the substance of his claim—'The plaintiff's claim is £1000 for money lent', 'The plaintiff's claim is for damages for breach of contract to employ the plaintiff as traveller', 'The plaintiff's claim is for damages for assault and false imprisonment', 'The plaintiff's claim is to recover a farm called Blackacre situate in the parish of Dale in the county of Kent'. We can no longer say that English law knows a certain number of actions and no more, or that every action has a writ appropriate to itself; the writ is always the same, the number of possible endorsements is as infinite as the number of unlawful acts and defaults which can give one man an action against another. All this is new. Formerly there were a certain number of writs which differed very markedly from each other. A writ of debt was very unlike a writ of trespass, and both were very unlike a writ of *mort d'ancestor* or a writ of right. A writ of debt was addressed to the sheriff; the sheriff is to command the defendant to pay to the plaintiff the alleged debt, or, if he will not do so, appear in court and answer why he has not done so. A writ of trespass is addressed to the sheriff; he is to attach the defendant to answer the plaintiff why with force and arms and against the king's peace he broke the plaintiff's close, or carried off his goods, or assaulted and beat him. A writ of *mort d'ancestor* bade the sheriff empanel a jury,

---

[1] Bract. fo. 413*b*.

or rather an assize, to answer a certain question formulated in the writ. A writ of right was directed not to the sheriff but to the feudal lord and bade him do right in his court between the demandant and the tenant. In each case the writ points to a substantially different procedure.

In the reign of Henry III Bracton had said *Tot erunt formulae brevium quot sunt genera actionum*.[1] There may be as many forms of action as there are causes of action. This suggests, what may seem true enough to us, that in order of logic Right comes before Remedy. There ought to be a remedy for every wrong; if some new wrong be perpetrated then a new writ may be invented to meet it. Just in Bracton's day it may have been possible to argue in this way; the king's court and the king's chancery— it was in the chancery that the writs were made—enjoyed a certain freedom which they were to lose as our parliamentary constitution became definitely established. A little later though the chancery never loses a certain power of varying the old formulas to suit new cases and this power was recognised by statute, still it is used but very cautiously. Court and chancery are conservative and Parliament is jealous of all that looks like an attempt to legislate without its concurrence. The argument from Right to Remedy is reversed and Bracton's saying is truer if we make it run *Tot erunt actiones quot sunt formulae brevium*—the forms of action are given, the causes of action must be deduced therefrom.

Of course we must not for one moment imagine that seventy years ago or in Blackstone's day litigation was really and truly carried on in just the same manner as that in which it was carried on in the days of Edward I. In the first place many of the forms of action had become obsolete: they were theoretically possible but were never used. In the second place the words 'really and truly' seem hardly applicable to any part of the procedure of the eighteenth century, so full was it of fictions contrived to get modern results out of medieval premises: writs were supposed to be issued which in fact never were issued, proceedings were supposed to be taken which in fact never were taken. Still these fictions had to be maintained, otherwise the whole system would have fallen to pieces; any one who would give a connected and rational account of the system was obliged—as Blackstone found himself obliged—to seek his starting point in a very remote age.

We will now briefly notice the main steps by which in the last century the forms of action were abolished. First we must observe that there was a well-known classification of the forms: they were (1) real, (2)

---

[1] Bract. fo. 413 b. A whole group of these forms is ascribed to Bracton's master, W. Raleigh—one might well have spoken of *actiones Raleighanae*.

personal, (3) mixed. I shall have to remark hereafter[1] that this classification had meant different things in different ages; Bracton would have called some actions personal which Blackstone would have called real or mixed. But at present it will be sufficient if we note Blackstone's definitions.[2]

Real actions, which concern real property only, are such whereby the plaintiff, here called the demandant, claims title to have any lands, or tenements, rents, commons, or other hereditaments in fee simple, fee tail or for term of life.

Personal actions are such whereby a man claims a debt, a personal duty, or damages in lieu thereof; and likewise, whereby a man claims a satisfaction in damages for some injury done to his person or property.

Mixed actions are suits partaking of the nature of the other two, wherein some real property is demanded, and also personal damages for a wrong sustained.

Now in 1833 the real and mixed actions were swept away at one fell swoop by the Real Property Limitation Act of that year, 3 and 4 Will. IV, c. 27, sec. 36. That section sets out the names of 60 actions and says that none of these and no other action real or mixed—except a writ of right of dower, a writ of dower, *unde nihil habet*, a *quare impedit*, or an ejectment—shall be brought after 31 December 1834. Practically for a very long time past the action of ejectment, which in its origin was distinctly a personal action, had been made to do duty for all or almost all the actions that were now to be abolished. The *quare impedit* had become the regular action for the trial of all disputes about advowsons, and, as ejectment was here inapplicable, this had to be spared. There were special reasons for saving the two writs of dower, since the doweress could not bring ejectment until her dower had been set out. But they were abolished in 1860 by the Common Law Procedure Act of that year (23 and 24 Vic., c. 126, sec. 26), and a new statutory action of a modern type was provided for the doweress. By the same Act, sec. 27, the old *quare impedit* was abolished and a new statutory action was put in its place.

Meanwhile in 1832 a partial assault had been made on the personal forms. The principal personal forms were these—Debt, Detinue, Covenant, Account, Trespass, Case, Trover, Assumpsit, Replevin. By 2 Will. IV, c. 39 (1832) 'Uniformity of Process Act'—the process in these personal actions was reduced to uniformity. The old original writs were abolished and a new form of writ provided. In this writ, however,

---

[1] See lecture V, below.   [2] Bl. *Comm.* III, 117, 118.

the plaintiff had to insert a mention of one of the known forms of action. Another heavy blow was struck in 1852 by the Common Law Procedure Act, 15 and 16 Vic., c. 76. It was expressly provided (sec. 3) that it should not be necessary to mention any form or cause of action in any writ of summons. But still this blow was not heavy enough—the several personal forms were still considered as distinct.

The final blow was struck by the Judicature Act of 1873 and the rules made thereunder, which came into force in 1875. This did much more than finally abolish the forms of actions known to the common law for it provided that equity and law should be administered concurrently. Since that time we have had what might fairly be called a Code of Civil Procedure. Of course we cannot here speak of the details of that Code; but you will not misunderstand me if I say that the procedure which it enjoins is comparatively formless. Of course there are rules, many rules.

We cannot say that whatever be the nature of the plaintiff's claim the action will always take the same course and pass through the same stages. For instance, when the plaintiff's claim falls within one of certain classes he can adopt a procedure[1] whereby when he has sworn positively to the truth of his claim the defendant can be shut out from defending the action at all unless he first makes oath to some good defence. So again there are cases in which either party can insist that the questions of fact, if any, shall be tried by jury; there are other cases in which there will be no trial by jury. Again, I must not allow you to think that a lawyer cannot do his client a great deal of harm by advising a bad or inappropriate course of procedure, though it is true that he cannot bring about a total shipwreck of a good cause so easily as he might have done some years ago. The great change gradually brought about and con- summated by the Judicature Acts is that the whole course of procedure in an action is not determined for good and all by the first step, by the original writ. It can no longer be said, as it might have been said in 1830 that we have about 72 forms of action, or as it might have been said in 1874 that we have about 12 forms of action. This is a different thing from saying that our English law no longer attempts to classify *causes* of action, on the contrary a rational, modern classification of causes of action is what we are gradually obtaining—but the forms of action belong to the past.

Since the Judicature Acts there are, of course, differences of proce- dure arising out of the character of the various actions, whether for

---

[1] Commonly called (from the Order which authorises this procedure) 'Going under Order XIV'.

divorce, probate of a will, specific performance of a contract: such differences there must be, but they can now be regarded as mere variations of one general theme—procedure in an action in the High Court of Justice. It was entirely otherwise in the Middle Ages, then lawyers say very little of the procedure in *an* action, very much of the procedure in some action of a particular kind, e.g. an assize of *mort d'ancestor* or an action of trespass. Knowledge of the procedure in the various forms of action is the core of English medieval jurisprudence. The Year Books are largely occupied by this. Glanvill plunges at once into the procedure in a writ of right. Bracton, with the Institutes scheme before him, gives about 100 folios to Persons and Things and about 350 to the law of Actions.

We can now attempt to draw some meagre outline of the general history of these forms of action, remembering, however, that a full history of them would be a full history of English private law.

Now I think that our first step should be to guard ourselves against the notion that from the very beginning it was the office of the king's own court or courts to provide a remedy for every wrong. This is a notion which we may but too easily adopt. In the first place it seems natural to us moderns, especially to us Englishmen, that in every decently governed country there should be some one tribunal, or some one definitely organized hierarchy of tribunals, fully competent to administer the whole law, to do right to every man in every case. In the second place it is true that in England such a scheme of centralised justice has existed from what, having regard to other countries, we may call a very remote time; it has existed for some five hundred years. Ever since Edward I's time, to name a date which is certainly not too recent, the law of England has to a very large extent been the law administered by the king's own courts, and to be without remedy in those courts has commonly been to be without any remedy at all. A moment's reflection will indeed remind us that we must use some such qualifying words as 'to a very large extent' when we lay down these wide propositions. Think for one moment of the copyholder, or of his predecessor the tenant in villeinage; he was not protected in his holding by the king's court, still to regard him as without rights would be a perversion of history. And then think of the ecclesiastical courts with their wide jurisdiction over matrimonial and testamentary causes; at least until the Reformation they were not in any sense the king's courts; their power was regarded as a spiritual power quite independent of the temporal power of the state. But in the third place we may be led into error by good masters. So long as the forms of action were still in use, it was difficult to tell the truth about their history. There they were, and it was the duty of judges and text writers to make the best of them, to treat them as though they formed a rational scheme provided all of a piece by some all-wise legislator. It was natural that lawyers should slip into the opinion that such had really been the case, to suppose, or to speak as though they supposed, that some great king (it matters not whether we call him Edward I or Edward the Confessor, Alfred or Arthur) had said to his wise men 'Go to now! a well ordered state should have a central tribunal, let us then with prudent forethought analyse all possible rights and provide a remedy for every imaginable wrong.' It was difficult to discover, difficult to tell, the truth, difficult to say that these forms of action belonged to very different ages, expressed very different and sometimes discordant theories of law, had been twisted and tortured to inappropriate uses, were the monuments of long-forgotten political struggles; above all it was difficult to say of them that they had their origin and their explanation in a time when the king's court was but one among many courts. But now, when the forms of action are gone, when we are no longer under any temptation to make them more rational than they were, the truth might be discovered and be told, and one part of the truth is assuredly this that throughout the early history of the forms of action there is an element of struggle, of struggle for jurisdiction. In order to understand them we must not presuppose a centralised system of justice, an omni-competent royal or national tribunal; rather we must think that the forms of action, the original writs, are the means whereby justice is becoming centralised, whereby the king's court is drawing away business from other courts.[1]

---

[1] As an example of the theory against which it is necessary to protest see Blackstone's account of Alfred's exploits, *Comm.* IV, 411: 'To him we owe that masterpiece of judicial polity, the subdivision of England into tithings and hundreds, if not into counties; all under the influence and administration of one supreme magistrate, the king; in whom as in a general reservoir, all the executive authority of the law was lodged, and from whom justice was dispensed to every part of the nation by distinct, yet communicating ducts and channels; which wise institution has been preserved for near a thousand years unchanged from Alfred's to the present time.'

LECTURE II

At the beginning of the twelfth century England was covered by an intricate network of local courts. In the first place there were the ancient courts of the shires and the hundreds, courts older than feudalism, some of them older than the English kingdom. Many of the hundred courts had fallen into private hands, had become the property of great men or great religious houses, and constant watchfulness was required on the king's part to prevent the sheriffs, the presidents of the county courts, from converting their official duties into patrimonial rights. Then again there were the feudal courts; the principle was establishing itself that tenure implied jurisdiction, that every lord who had tenants enough to form a court might hold a court of and for his tenants. Above all these rose the king's own court. It was destined to increase, while all the other courts were destined to decrease; but we must not yet think of it as a court of first instance for all litigants; rather it, like every other court, had its limited sphere of jurisdiction. Happily the bounds of that sphere were never very precisely formulated; it could grow and it grew. The cases which indisputably fell within it we may arrange under three heads. In the first place there were the pleas of the crown (*placita coronae*), matters which in one way or another especially affected the king, his crown and dignity. All infringements of the king's own proprietary rights fell under this head, and the king was a great proprietor. But in addition to this almost all criminal justice was gradually being claimed for the king; such justice was a profitable source of revenue, of forfeitures, fines and amercements. The most potent of the ideas which operated for this result was the idea of the king's peace. Gradually this peace—which at one time was conceived as existing only at certain times, in certain places, and in favour of certain privileged persons, covering the king's coronation days, the king's highways, the king's servants and those to whom he had granted it by his hand or his seal— was extended to cover all times, the whole realm, all men. Then again when Henry II introduced the new procedure against criminals by way of presentment or indictment—placed this method of public or communal accusation by the side of the old private accusation or appeal—he very carefully kept this new procedure in the hands of his justices and his sheriffs. Subsequent changes diminished even the power of the sheriffs, and before the twelfth century was out all that could be called very serious criminal justice had become the king's, to be exercised only by his justices or by a few very highly privileged lords to whom it had been expressly granted. With the history of criminal law we have here no great concern; only let us notice that it is in this field that the centralising process goes on most rapidly and that the idea of the king's peace is by no means exhausted when all grave crimes are conceived as committed against the peace of our lord the king; the same idea will in course of time bring within the cognizance of the royal court every, the slightest, wrongful application of physical force.

Secondly, even had feudal theory and feudal practice gone unchecked, the king, as the ultimate lord of all lords, would have been able to claim for his own court a certain supervisory power over all lower courts. If a man could not get justice out of his immediate lord he might go to that lord's lord, and so in the last resort to the king. We must not here introduce the notion of an 'appeal' from court to court, for that is a modern notion. In old times he who goes from court to court does not go there merely to get a mistake put right, to get an erroneous judgment reversed; he goes there to lodge a complaint against his lord or the judges of his lord's court, to accuse his lord of having made default in justice (*propter defectum justiciae*), to accuse the judges of having pronounced a false judgment; he challenges his judges and they may have to defend their judgment by their oaths or by their bodies. Still the king has here an acknowledged claim to be the supreme judge over all judges, and this claim can be pressed and extended, for if it profits the king it profits the great mass of the people also.

Thirdly, even the extremest theory of feudalism would have to allow the king to do justice between his own tenants in chief; however little more a king may be he is at the very least a feudal lord with tenants, and may hold, and ought to hold, a court of them and for them.

Had the worst come to the worst the king might have claimed these things, jurisdiction over his own immediate tenants, jurisdiction when all lower lords have made default, a few specially royal pleas known as pleas of the crown. To this he might have been reduced by feudalism. We ought not indeed to think that in England his justice was ever strictly pent within these limits; the kingship established by conquest was too strong for that, still he could not exceed these limits without a struggle. That his court should fling open its doors to all litigants, should hold itself out to be a court for all cases great and small, for all men, whosesoever men they be, is a principle that only slowly gains ground. Despite all that was done by Henry II, despite the ebb of feudalism, we can hardly say that this principle is admitted before the coronation of Edward I. In the middle of the thirteenth century, Bracton, a royal judge, whose work constantly displays strong anti-feudal leanings, who has no mean idea of his master's power, who holds the theory that all justice is in the last resort the king's, that it is merely lack of time and strength that prevents the king from hearing every cause in person, is none the less forced to make something very like an apology for the activity of the king's court—one class of cases must come before it for one reason, another for another, but some reason, some excuse there must be; it cannot yet be assumed as an obvious rule that every one whose rights have been infringed can bring his case before the king's justices.

A little must be said about the constitution and the procedure of these communal and feudal courts. In the courts of the shire and the hundred the judgments were made by the suitors of the court, those freeholders who were bound to attend its periodic sittings. The court was presided over by the sheriff, or if the hundred was one that had fallen into private hands, by the lord's steward; but the judgments were made by the suitors; they were the *judicatores* of the court; it is not improbable that in English they were called the dooms-men of the court. So in the feudal courts, the lord's steward presided, but the tenants who owed suit of court were the dooms-men. It was for them to make the judgments, and it is probable that if they differed in opinion the judgment of the majority prevailed. But this judgment was not like a modern judgment. In modern German books dealing with ancient procedure we find the startling proposition that judgment preceded proof; it was a judgment that one party or the other to the litigation was to prove his case. Now when in our own day we speak of proof we think of an attempt made by each litigant to convince the judge, or the jurors, of the truth of the facts that he has alleged; he who is successful in this competition has proved his case. But in old times proof was not an attempt to convince the judges; it was an appeal to the supernatural, and very commonly a unilateral act. The common modes of proof are oaths and ordeals. It is adjudged, for example, in an action for debt that the defendant do prove his assertion that he owes nothing by his own oath and the oaths of a certain number of compurgators, or oath-helpers. The defendant must then solemnly swear that he owes nothing, and his oath-helpers must swear that his oath is clean and unperjured. If they safely get through this ceremony, punctually repeating the right formula, there is an end of the case; the plaintiff, if he is hardy enough to go on, can only do so by bringing a new charge, a criminal charge of perjury against them.

They have not come there to convince the court, they have not come there to be examined and cross-examined like modern witnesses, they have come there to bring upon themselves the wrath of God if what they say be not true. This process is known in England as 'making one's law'; a litigant who is adjudged to prove his case in this way is said to 'wage his law' (*vadiare legem*), when he finds security that on a future day he will bring compurgators and perform this solemnity; then when on the appointed day he comes and performs that ceremony with success, he is said to 'make his law' (*facere legem*). An ordeal is still more obviously an appeal to the supernatural; the judgment of God is given; the burning iron spares the innocent, the water rejects the guilty. Or again the court adjudges that there must be trial by battle; the appellor charges the appellee with a crime, the appellee gives him the lie; the demandant's champion swears that he saw the demandant seised of the land, and is ready to prove this by his body; the wit of man is at fault in presence of a flat contradiction; God will show the truth. It is hard for us to say how this ancient procedure worked in practice, hard to tell how easy it was to get oath-helpers who would swear falsely, hard to tell how much risk there was in an ordeal. The rational element of law must, it would seem, have asserted itself in the judgment which decided how and by whom the proof should be given; the jurisprudence of the old courts must have been largely composed of the answers to this question; and some parts of it are being recovered, for example we can see that even before the Norman Conquest the man who has been often accused has to go to the ordeal instead of being allowed to purge himself with oath-helpers. But the point now to be seized is that the history of the forms of action presupposes this background of ancient courts with their unprofessional judges, their formal, supernatural modes of proof.

In its constitution and in its procedure the king's court is ahead of the other courts. Theoretically, from the Conquest onwards, it may be a feudal court, one in which all the king's tenants in chief, or such at least of them as are deemed barons, are entitled and bound to sit under the presidency of the king, his high steward or his chief justiciar. To this day the king's highest court of all is the assembly of the lords spiritual and temporal. But practically a small knot of trained administrators, prelates and barons, becomes the king's court for ordinary judicial purposes. The reforms of Henry II, the new actions invented in his reign, brought an ever-increasing mass of litigation before the royal court. It became more and more a group of men professionally learned in the law. Gradually, as is well known, this group breaks up into three courts, there are the three courts of common law, the King's Bench, Common Bench, and Exchequer. This process is not complete until Edward I's reign; but we may say that for a century before this the king's court for ordinary judicial purposes has been no feudal court of tenants in chief, but a court of professional justices; the justices of Henry III's time are often men who have had a long education in the subordinate offices of the court and the chancery.

As to procedure, all the old formal modes of proof have been known in the king's court. It made use of the ordeal until that ancient process was abolished by the Lateran Council of 1215. Trial by battle, as we all know, was not abolished until 1819,[1] and wager of law was not abolished until 1833.[2] For a very long time before this any practical talk of these barbarisms had been very rare, and for a still longer time pent within ever-narrowing limits; still, if we are to understand the history of the forms of action, we must be mindful of these things; a long chapter in that history might be entitled 'Dodges to evade Wager of Battle', a still longer chapter, 'Dodges to evade Wager of Law'. We must not suppose that the unreasonableness of these archaic institutions was suddenly perceived; the cruelties of the *peine forte et dure* had their origin in the sentiment that trial by jury is not a fair mode of trial save for those who have voluntarily consented to it; the remembrance of the ordeal was dear to the people; they would 'swim a witch' long centuries after the Lateran Council; so late as 1376 we find that wager of law is still popular with the commons of England, they pray that there may be wager of law in the Exchequer as in the other courts.[3] But to a very great extent the early history of the forms of action is the history of a new procedure gradually introduced, the procedure which in course of time becomes trial by jury. It would be needless to repeat here what has been sufficiently said elsewhere about the first germs of the jury. The Frankish kings, perhaps assuming to themselves the rights of the Roman fiscus, had placed themselves outside the ancient formal procedure of the popular courts, had sought to preserve and enforce their royal rights by compelling the inhabitants of the district, or a representative body of such inhabitants, to swear that they would tell the truth as to the nature and extent of these rights. Further, they gave or sold this privilege to specially favoured persons, especially to the churches which were under their patronage. The favoured person, if possessions were attacked, need not defend them by battle, or ordeal, or any of the ancient modes of

---

[1] 59 Geo. III, c. 46.   [2] 3 and 4 Will. IV, c. 42, sec. 13.
[3] Rot. Parl. III, 337.

proof, but might have an inquest of neighbours sworn to tell the truth about the matter in hand. Immediately after the Norman Conquest we find that this procedure has been introduced into England, and it is employed on a magnificent scale. Domesday Book is the record of the verdicts of bodies of neighbours sworn to tell the truth, and its main object is the ascertainment and preservation of the king's rights. Very soon after this we find the inquest or jury employed in the course of litigation; for instance, in a suit touching the rights of the Church of Ely the Conqueror commands that those who best know how the lands lay in the days of the Confessor shall be sworn to tell the truth about them; so a number of the good folk of Sandwich are sworn to tell the truth about a certain ship, and they testifying in favour of the Abbot of St Augustine's, the abbot is 'reseised' of the ship. The right to a jury makes its appearance as a royal prerogative, a prerogative, the benefit of which the king can give or sell to those who obtain his grace. We see traces of this origin even at a very late time; it is an established maxim that one cannot wage one's law against the king. In an action for debt upon simple contract, were the plaintiff a subject, the defendant would be allowed to purge himself with oath-helpers in the ancient way, but when the king is plaintiff he must submit to trial by jury.

In the competition of courts, therefore, the king's court has a marked advantage; to say nothing of its power to enforce its judgments it has, for those who can purchase or otherwise obtain such a favour, a comparatively rational procedure. As yet, indeed, trial by jury is far from being what it became in later times; the jurors are not 'judges of fact', they are witnesses; but they are not like the witnesses and the compurgators of the old procedure; they are not brought in by the party to swear up to a set form of words in support of his case, they are summoned as impartial persons by a royal officer, and they swear to tell the truth, whatever the truth may be. This is the procedure, far more rational than battle, or ordeal, or wager of law, which the king's court has at its command when it begins to bid against the communal and feudal courts. If for a moment we may refer to Roman law, we may say that the history of English law does not begin with the formulary system—that is the product of the twelfth and thirteenth centuries—at the back of the formulary system are *legis actiones*.

LECTURE III

This morning I shall attempt a sketch in brief outline of the order in which the different forms of action are developed. But first I ought to say that I do not know that any such attempt has yet been made, and that, as I must be very brief, I shall be compelled perhaps to state in too dogmatic a fashion some conclusions that are disputable. To this I must add that some things that I say this morning may seem unintelligible. I hope to make my meaning clearer in subsequent lectures. We must break up our history into periods.

I. 1066–1154. The first of these periods would end with the great reforms of Henry II. Litigation of an ordinary kind still takes place chiefly in the communal and feudal courts; even the king's court may be considered as a feudal court, a court of and for the king's tenants in chief, though a professional element is apparent in it since the king keeps around him a group of trained administrators. His court is concerned chiefly with (1) the pleas of the Crown, i.e. cases in which royal rights are concerned, (2) litigation between the king's tenants in chief—for such tenants it is the proper feudal court, (3) complaints of default of justice in lower courts. From time to time he interferes with ordinary litigation; at the instance of a litigant he issues a writ commanding a feudal lord or a sheriff to do justice, or he sends out some of his officers to hear the case in the local courts, or again he evokes the case before his own court. Such interferences cannot be secured for nothing; they may be considered as luxuries, and men may be expected to pay for them; the litigant does not exactly buy the king's justice, but he buys the king's aid, and the king has valuable commodities for sale; the justice that he does is more peremptory than the justice that can be had elsewhere, and the process of empanelling a body of neighbour-witnesses, the process which in course of time will become trial by jury, is a royal monopoly. The writs of this period, so far as we can judge from the specimens that have been preserved, were penned to meet the particular circumstances of the particular cases without any studious respect for precedent. We do indeed come upon writs which seem as it were to foretell the fixed formulas of a later age; we are sometimes inclined to say 'This is a writ of right, that a writ of debt, that a writ of trespass'; but we have little reason to suppose that the work of issuing writs had as yet become a matter of routine entrusted to subordinate officers whose duty was to copy from models. Perhaps no writ went out without the approval of the king himself or the express direction of his justiciar or chancellor; and probably every writ was a purchasable favour.

II. 1154–89. The legislative activity of Henry II's reign marks a second period. Under Henry II the exceptional becomes normal. He places royal justice at the disposal of anyone who can bring his case within a certain formula. From the end of his reign we have Glanvill's book, and we see already a considerable apparatus of writs which are at the disposal of litigants or of such litigants as will pay for them; they have assumed distinct forms, forms which they will preserve until the nineteenth century, and probably the issue of them is fast becoming a matter of routine; each writ is the beginning of a particular form of action. Let us look at some of these writs.

First the Writ of Right. There is good reason to believe that Henry, in some ordinance lost to us, laid down the broad principle that no man need answer for his freehold without royal writ. Everyone therefore who demands freehold land must obtain a writ; otherwise his adversary will not be bound to answer him. This principle of vast importance is laid down clearly enough in the book ascribed to Glanvill. On the other hand it seems to be a new principle; we have little cause to believe that it was in force before Henry's day or that it ever was law in Normandy; more than once we find it connected with another rule which we also ascribe to Henry, a rule of which much must be said hereafter, namely, that no one is to be disseised of his freehold unjustly and without judgment, that every one so disseised has an action (called an Assize of Novel Disseisin) before the king's own justices. In 1207 King John sent a writ to the people of Ireland in which he coupled these two rules: 'We will that none shall disseise you of your free tenements unjustly and without a judgment, and that you shall not be impleaded for your free tenements without our writ or that of our justiciar.'[1] We find Bracton again coupling these two principles: no one shall be disseised of his free tenement without a judgment, nor need he answer for it without the king's command and writ.[2] Of these two principles the one is that of the great possessory action, the Assize of Novel Disseisin, the other is of wider import, no action for freehold can be begun without the king's writ, or if it be so begun the person who is in possession need not answer. But let us observe that there is a close connection between the two: both can be represented as measures for the protection of posses-

[1] Rot. Pat. 76; Select Pleas in Manorial Courts, I, liv.
[2] Bract. fo. 161: 'Nemo debet sine judicio disseisiri de libero tenemento suo, nec respondere sine praecepto domini Regis nec sine brevi.'

sion, of seisin of free tenement; such possession is to be protected against extrajudicial force; but this is not enough, it is to be protected also against irresponsible justice; he who is seised shall remain seised until some judgment is given against him in accordance with the king's writ. Henry did not ordain, could not have ordained, that all litigation respecting free tenements should take place in the king's court; such a measure would have been too open an abrogation of the first principle of feudalism. It seems very possible that he was able to represent the great step that he took as no interference with proprietary rights but a mere protection of possession, while the protection of possession was intimately associated with the maintenance of the king's peace which was now conceived as surrounding all men.

At any rate this principle took firm root in English law: no one need answer for his freehold without the king's writ. This does not mean that every action for freehold must be begun in the king's court; far from it. Suppose that A claims land that B holds, and that it is common ground between them that the land ought to be held of C; then undoubtedly C's court is the proper tribunal. But B need not answer unless A obtains a writ. The writ which A will obtain if he is asserting title to the land will be a writ addressed by the king to C in this form: 'I command you that without delay you hold full right to A (i.e. do full justice to A) concerning a virgate of land in Middleton which he claims to hold of you by such and such a free service, and unless you do it my sheriff of Northamptonshire shall do it, that I may hear no further complaint about this matter for default of justice.' Such a writ is called a writ of right (*breve de recto tenendo*), and because it is an open writ and not sealed up, as some writs are, it is a writ of right patent (*breve de recto patens*).[1] If, however, the demandant claims to hold the land of the king as tenant in chief such a writ is out of place; there is no mesne lord to whom it can be directed; the proper tribunal is the king's own court. So the writ takes a different form.[1] It is directed to the sheriff: 'Command B that justly and without delay he render to A a hide of land in Middleton, whereof A complains that B unjustly deforces him, and if he will not do it, summon him that he be before my justices at such a place and time to answer why he has not done it'; the tenant of the land must give it up to the demandant or answer in the king's court. In saying that this simple writ, this *Praecipe quod reddat*, was only used when the demandant claimed to hold of the king as tenant in chief, we have been

---

[1] The Writ of Right Patent and the *Praecipe quod reddat* are printed among the Select Writs after these lectures.

guilty of some inaccuracy. Glanvill tells us that such a writ is issued when the king pleases; Henry II was not very careful of the interests of mesne lords and would send a *Praecipe quod reddat* to the sheriff when a Writ of Right addressed to the lord would have been more in harmony with feudal principles. But this was regarded as a tyrannical abuse and was struck at by a clause of the Great Charter[1]—the writ called *Praecipe* shall not be issued for the future so as to deprive any free man of his court; a proprietary action for land must be begun in the lord's court; the *Praecipe quod reddat* is only in place when the demandant claims to hold in chief of the king, in other words when it is a *Praecipe in capite*. We have therefore to distinguish between two forms of the proprietary action for land, that begun in the lord's court by Writ of Right, that begun in the king's court by *Praecipe in capite*; but in course of time the term 'Writ of Right' gains a somewhat extended sense and is used so as to include the *Praecipe in capite*. This is due to the contrast between possession and property, or, to use the terms then current, between 'seisin' and 'right'. The *Praecipe in capite* is the beginning of a pro-prietary action, one in which the demandant relies on right, not merely on seisin, and so it may be called a writ of right.

Now the action commenced by Writ of Right was an extremely slow and solemn affair—so at least it was considered in after ages when it could be compared with more rapid actions. It involved a great number of delays (*dilaciones*), of adjournments from term to term. Among the causes which in course of time have rendered justice more rapid we must reckon not merely good roads, organised postal service, railways, electric telegraphs, but also the principle that men can hand over their litigation and their other business to be done for them by agents, whose acts will be their acts. Rapid justice may nowadays be fair justice, because if a litigant cannot be present in court in his own person, he may well be there by his attorney and his counsel. But this principle that every suitor may appear in court by attorney is one that has grown up by slow degrees, and, like so many other principles which may seem to us principles of 'natural justice', it first appears as a royal prerogative; the king can empower a man to appoint an attorney.[2] But so long as litigants have to

---

[1] Magna Carta (1215), c. 34: Breve quod vocatur Praecipe non fiat alicui de aliquo tenemento unde liber homo amittere possit curiam suam.

[2] Fitz. *Nat. Brev.* 25: Bl. *Comm.* III, 25. Blackstone adds 'This is still the law in criminal cases, and an idiot cannot to this day appear by attorney, but in person, for he hath not discretion to enable him to appoint a proper substitute: and upon his being brought before the court in so defenceless a condition, the

appear in person justice must often be slow if it is to be just; the sick man cannot come, so one must wait until he is well; one must give the crusader a chance of returning. But one cannot wait for ever; that would be unfair to the other party; so a great deal of law is evolved as to the excuses for non-appearance, in technical language the *essoins*, that a man may proffer. This is one of the causes which raise high the barriers between the various forms of action. In the action begun by Writ of Right, which will finally deprive one of the parties of all claim to the land, the essoins are manifold; a litigant can generally delay the action for year and day by betaking himself to his bed;[1] in other actions so many essoins are not admissible.

It is worthy of notice that the Praecipe for land, the Writ of Debt, and many other writs afterwards invented, are not in the first instance writs instituting litigation; that, according to their tenor, is not their primary object. The king through his sheriff commands a man to do something, bids him give up the land that he wrongfully withholds, or pay the debt that he owes. Only in case of neglecting to obey this command is there to be any litigation. May we not say then that the 'cause of action' in the king's court is in theory not the mere wrong done to the plaintiff or demandant by keeping him out of his land or neglecting to pay money due to him, but this wrong coupled with disobedience to the king's command? There can I think be little doubt that such a conception was operative in the growth of royal jurisdiction. If we look back at the *Leges Henrici* we find that among the rights which the king has over all men, among the pleas of the crown, stands the *placitum brevium vel praeceptorum ejus contemptorum*, any action we may say founded on a contempt of his writs or commands.[2] The wrong done to the plaintiff or demandant is a breach of law and a wrong which should be redressed somewhere; but it is the contempt of the king's writ which makes it a wrong which should be redressed in the king's court; in the language of the old English laws there has been an 'over-

---

judges are bound to take care of his interests, and they shall admit the best plea in his behalf that anyone present can suggest.'

[1] Some care was taken to see that his excuse was not too unreal. Four knights were sent to visit him, to award whether he had 'malum transiens' or a 'languor'—which was what he needed—after consideration of whether they found him 'vagantem per rura' or 'in bed as befits a man making such excuse, unbooted, unbreeched and ungirt, or even naked which is more' (decalceatum, et sine braccis et decinctum, vel forte nudum, quod plus est). Bracton, fo. 356 *b*.

[2] Leg. Hen. Prim. c. 10.

seeness' or 'overhearness' of the king which must be emended; the deforciant of land or of a debt has not merely to give up the land or pay the debt, he is at the mercy of our lord the king and is amerced accordingly.

The mode of trial appropriate to the Writ of Right has been trial by battle. We may reckon as the second of Henry's reforms in civil procedure that he gave to the tenant the option of another mode of trial; instead of the judicial combat he might put himself upon the grand assize of our lord the king. The text of this ordinance, this grand assize (*magna assisa*) we have not got. Glanvill's account of it is well known— 'The grand assize is a royal boon conceded to the people by the clemency of the prince on the advice of his nobles whereby wholesome provision is made for the lives of men and the integrity of the state, so that in defending the right which every one possesses in his free tenement they may refuse the doubtful issue of battle ... This institution proceeds from the highest equity; for the right which after many and long delays can hardly be said to be proved by battle is more rapidly and more fitly demonstrated by this beneficent ordinance.'[1] If the tenant (that is, the party attacked by the Writ of Right) claims the benefit of this ordinance, puts himself on the grand assize of our lord the king, the action is removed out of the lord's court and is brought before the king's justices; four knights of the neighbourhood are summoned to choose twelve other knights who are sworn to say, to 'recognise' (*recognoscere*), whether the demandant or the tenant has the greater right to the land. The name 'grand assize' is transferred from the ordinance to the institution that it creates; these twelve recognitors are 'a grand assize'. It is best not to call them a 'jury', for though we see here one stage, and a very important stage, in the growth of trial by jury, still in many respects trial by the grand assize to the last day of its existence—and such a trial was possible in 1834[2]—remained a distinct thing from trial by jury. We observe for instance that the recognitors were sworn to tell the truth not about mere facts—the separation of questions of fact from questions of law belongs to a later day—but to tell the truth about rights, to say whether A or B has the greater right (*jus majus*). We may notice also that here again the king is interfering in favour of possession; it is not either party that can claim this royal boon, it is only the tenant, the man in possession; no such grace is shown to demandants, they can be compelled to stake their claims on the issue of a combat.

[1] Glanv. II, 7; Stubbs, *Const. Hist.* I, 615.
[2] 3 and 4 Will. IV, c. 27, sec. 36.

Now the possessory assizes: In sharp contrast to the action begun by Writ of Right there now stand three possessory actions, the three Assizes of Novel Disseisin, Mort d'Ancestor, and Darrein Presentment. There can, I suppose, be but little doubt that the notion of a definitely possessory action may be traced to the Roman interdicts, through that *actio spolii* which the canonists were gradually developing. But the English and Norman assizes—for we find these actions in Normandy as well as in England, and there is some reason for thinking that they are a little older in Normandy than in England—have many features which are distinctly not Roman and not Canonical. Roman law and Canon law may have afforded suggestions but hardly models. We will look at these three assizes.

(*a*) The principle of the Novel Disseisin is this, that if one person has unjustly and without a judgment disseised another of his free tenement, and the latter, the disseisee, at once complains of this to the king he shall be put back into seisin by the judgment of the king's court. The procedure is this, the plaintiff lodges his complaint, at once a writ is issued bidding the sheriff summon twelve good and lawful men of the neighbourhood to 'recognise' (*recognoscere*) before the king's justices whether B unjustly and without a judgment disseised A of his free tenement within the time limited for the bringing of an assize. If this body of recognitors, this assize—for the procedure is called an assize and the twelve neighbours are called an assize—answers 'yes' to the question thus formulated in the writ, then the plaintiff, the disseisee, will be put back into seisin.

The formula of the Novel Disseisin contains terms which in course of time will give birth to a great deal of law; the successful plaintiff must have been disseised of his free tenement unjustly; but what is seisin, what is a free tenement, when is a man disseised unjustly ? Postponing any discussion of these terms we can still notice that the action has a narrow definite scope. It can be brought only by a disseisee against a disseisor. It cannot, for example, be brought by the heir of the disseisee, or against the heir of the disseisor. Again, disseisin implies more than a wrongful assumption of possession, it implies a turning of some one out of possession; to enter on land of which no one is seised is no disseisin; if, for example, on the death of a rightful tenant a stranger enters before the heir enters, that stranger is no disseisor. This Assize of Novel Disseisin is no remedy for the recovery of land to which one is entitled; to speak roughly it is an action competent to a person who has been turned out of possession, and competent against the person who turned him out. It decides nothing as to proprietary right. In a Writ of Right the demandant claims the land as his *right* and inheritance (*ut jus et hereditatem suam*); he has to allege that he or some ancestor of his was seised as of right (*ut de jure*); no such allegation is made by the plaintiff in the Novel Disseisin; it is enough that he has been seised and disseised, and of right there is no talk. Consequently this action, if the plaintiff be successful, in no way decides that the plaintiff has better right than the disseisor; the plaintiff is put back into seisin, but after all the disseisor may be the true owner; he may at once bring a Writ of Right against his hitherto successful adversary; the court will help him to his own though it has punished him for helping himself.

Then again this action must be brought within a limited term; the complaint must be one of recent dispossession (*de nova disseisina*). In England this term was fixed from time to time by royal ordinance. When Glanvill wrote the action had to be brought since the king's last passage to Normandy, an event which must have been quite recent. In Normandy we find a rule which has a curiously archaic sound; the plaintiff must have been seised when the last harvest was reaped. The principle of the Novel Disseisin if it has one root in the Interdicts seems to have another in the ancient notion, very prominent in Norman law, that the man engaged in agricultural operations enjoys a special peace.

Then again the Novel Disseisin was a very summary action, *ut per summariam cognitionem absque magna juris solemnitate quasi per compendium negotium terminetur*,[1] says Bracton. In course of time these assizes became very bywords for dilatoriness; but I see no reason to doubt that in the twelfth century their procedure was quite as rapid as was compatible with the elementary rules of justice.[2] No essoin was permitted; no pleading was necessary; the question for the recognitors was formulated in the writ which summoned them; there could be no voucher to warranty of any one not named in the writ; the first process against the defendant was not a mere summons but an attachment; it was even enough to attach his bailiff. When Bracton tells us that the invention of this action had cost pains, that it was *multis vigiliis excogitata et inventa*,[3] we can believe him; a splendid success awaited it.

(*b*) The principle of the Assize of Mort d'Ancestor (*assisa de morte antecessoris*) is this, that when a person has died seised as of fee—*ut de*

---

[1] Bract. fo. 164*b*.   [2] See Glanv. XIII, 38.
[3] Bract. fo. 164*b*.

feodo—his heir ought to be seised, and that if any other person obtains seisin before the heir, that person shall be turned out by the judgment of the court in favour of the heir. The procedure is somewhat like that of the Novel Disseisin, though not so summary. The questions for the recognitors are formulated in the original writ and are these, 'Whether M, the father, mother, brother, sister, uncle or aunt of A, the plaintiff, was seised in his demesne as a fee of the land in question now held by X, whether M died within the time limited for bringing the action, and whether A is M's next heir.' If all these questions are answered in the plaintiff's favour then he is put in seisin.

The action is regarded as distinctly possessory in this sense that it decides nothing about proprietary right. It is necessary that the plaintiff's ancestor should have been seised, that he should have been seised 'as of fee', that is to say, that he should not have been seised as a mere tenant for life or the like, that he should have been seised 'in demesne', that is that he should, in our modern terms, have been seised of the land itself and not merely of a seignory over lands held of him by another; but it is by no means necessary that he should have been seised as of right; of right there is no talk at all. It follows A may recover from X in a Mort d'Ancestor, while X having better right than A will recover from him in a proprietary action, in a Writ of Right.

Seisin, we may observe, is not conceived as a descendible right. The heir of one who died seised is not at once in seisin; he must enter on the land before he will be seised. If during the interval a stranger enters, that stranger will be no disseisor. Had seisin been considered as a descendible right there would have been no place for the Mort d'Ancestor, for its sphere would have been covered by the Novel Disseisin. On the other hand seisin (unless the person seised claims but a temporary estate as tenant for life or the like) does found or generate a descendible right—a person who dies seised ought to be succeeded by his heir and by no other, and if any other person obtains seisin, he shall be put out of it; if he thinks that he has better right than the heir because better right than the ancestor, let him bring his action; help himself he shall not. In course of time (but this as I think belongs to a later period) it is even said that on the death of one who dies seised as of fee, his heir is at once 'seised in law' though he is not 'seised in deed' until he enters; this means that during the interval he has some, though by no means all, of the advantages of seisin. The older notion seems to be that though seisin is not descendible it does beget a descendible right, and at any rate the Mort d'Ancestor gives us this important principle that the heir of one who dies seised ought to be put in seisin and remain seised until some one else proves a better right in due course of law.

But we have mis-stated the rule implied in this assize in a point worth mentioning. In order that the plaintiff may be successful, it is essential not merely that he should be the heir of the dead person, but that he should be the son, daughter, brother, sister, nephew, niece of that person. The Mort d'Ancestor lies only on the death of a father, mother, brother, sister, uncle or aunt. The dead man's heir happens to be his grandson; that grandson cannot bring an assize. Why so? We must, as I think, answer that the limitation is quite unprincipled; that legislators deal with obvious cases and leave rarer cases unprovided for, either because they are forgotten or because they are troublesome. The remark is worth making for there are many things in the history of our law, and, I should suppose, in the history of every body of law, which can only be explained by that *vis inertiae* which makes against legal reforms. And let us observe what happens. The formula of the Mort d'Ancestor is never enlarged; but new actions are invented to meet the omitted cases. This happened it would seem under Henry III in or about 1237. The actions known as actions of Aiel, Besaiel and Cosinage; if the dead man was the grandfather (aiel), or great-grandfather (besaiel), or cousin of the heir, that heir was to have an action which would do for him what the Mort d'Ancestor would have done had the degree of kinship between them been closer. But there was difficulty about giving these actions; the feudal lords resisted the endeavour on the ground that business which properly belonged to their courts was thus attracted to the king's court. Bracton has to argue that the new actions are purely possessory, that they are mere necessary supplements of the Assize of Mort d'Ancestor and that they do no wrong to the lords.[1] The story is instructive; it illustrates what I may call the irrational element in the history of the forms of action, the element of chance in legal history. The result is that a mere accident of no juristic value, the mere accident that the degree of kinship between heir and ancestor is near or remote, decides whether the heir shall have a twelfth century remedy by Assize of Mort d'Ancestor or a thirteenth century remedy by a Writ of Cosinage; the procedure in these two actions is substantially different, the one is more archaic than the other and yet the same principle of law covers them both.

(c) The third of the possessory Assizes is that of Darrein Presentment

[1] Bracton's Note Book, pl. 1215; Bract. fo. 281.

or last presentation (*de ultima presentatione*). It deals with a matter which was of great value in the middle ages and which gave rise to an enormous amount of litigation, the advowsons of churches. If a man claimed property in an advowson his remedy was by a Writ of Right closely resembling the *Praecipe in capite* for lands. The king had asserted successfully both as against the feudal lords and as against the ecclesiastical tribunals that all litigation about the right to present to churches must take place in his court. The Writ of Right of Advowson was the proprietary remedy; but here also a possessory action was needed and was instituted. The procedure closely resembled that of the two other possessory assizes though it was not quite so summary as that of the Novel Disseisin. Its principle was this: if a church is vacant the person who last presented or his heir is entitled to present; if any other person conceives that he has better right, he must bring his action and recover the advowson, but until he has done this it is for the person who last presented, or his heir, to present again. The question addressed to the recognitors is this—Who was the patron who in time of peace presented the last parson to this church? The act of successfully presenting a parson to a church was regarded as a seisin, a possession of the advowson; the man who has performed that act is seised of the advowson and when the church again falls vacant, it is for him or, if he be dead, his heir to present another parson, provided that in the meantime he has not been deprived of his seisin by judgment. The need of some rapid procedure to meet cases in which two persons claimed the right to present to the same church was great; while an action by Writ of Right of Advowson was dragging on its wearisome length, the parishioners would be left as sheep without a shepherd or the bishop would step in and deprive both litigants of the coveted piece of patronage; therefore let him who has presented once present again until some one has proved a better right in due course of law.

(*d*) A fourth Assize must here be mentioned, the Assize *Utrum* or Writ *Juris Utrum*. It reminds us that in the twelfth century royal justice had to contend not only with feudal justice, but also with ecclesiastical justice. If land has been dedicated to ecclesiastical purposes, has been given in free alms, in frank almoign (*libera elemosyna*) the church claims cognisance of all disputes relating to that land. The question is what to do when one party to the litigation asserts that the land is held in free alms, and so within the sphere of the ecclesiastical tribunals, while the other asserts that it is lay fee. This difficulty gave occasion for one of the very earliest applications of what in a loose sense we may call trial by jury. One of the Constitutions of Clarendon (1164)[1] is to this effect: 'If a dispute arises between a clerk and a layman, or a layman and a clerk about any tenement which the clerk asserts to belong to free alms, the layman to lay fee, it shall be decided on a recognition of twelve lawful men by the judgment of the king's chief justiciar, whether (*utrum*) the tenement belongs to free alms or to lay fee. And if it be "recognised" to belong to free alms, the plea shall proceed in the ecclesiastical court, but if it be lay fee then the plea shall proceed in the king's court, unless both parties claim to hold of the same bishop or baron, in which case it shall proceed in the [feudal] court of that bishop or baron. And the person who is in seisin shall not lose his seisin on account of that "recognition" until the plea be tried out.' We see here a preliminary procedure; it is to settle nothing about right, nothing even about seisin, it is merely to settle the competence of tribunals, to decide whether the action shall proceed before a spiritual or a temporal tribunal. But it had a very peculiar history. Subsequent changes in the relation between church and state, changes which in this instance extended the sphere of the lay courts at the expense of that of the Courts Christian, gave this assize a new turn. Still keeping its old form of an assize it became a proprietary remedy in the king's court for a parson who wished to recover the lands of his church; it became 'the parson's writ of right'. We have constantly to remember this, that an action instituted for one purpose in one age comes to be used for another purpose in another age.[2]

These were all the actions which in England permanently took the name and form of assizes. By saying that they took the form of assizes I mean that the original writ directed the summoning of a body of recognitors to give sworn answer to a particular question formulated in that writ. In Normandy there were some other assizes, and these may for a short while have been used in England; but the germ of trial by jury having once been introduced in these formal assizes, it began to spread outside their limits, to take a new shape and become susceptible of free development. We learn from Glanvill that certain incidental questions may be raised in an action which will be decided by the oath of twelve men. For example, A brings an Assize of Mort d'Ancestor against B, who is an infant; now it is a rule of law that an infant during his infancy need never answer for land of which his ancestor died seised

---

[1] Cap. 9.

[2] *Très Ancien Coutumier*, c. 57; Const. Clarend. c. 9; Glanv. XIII, 23; Bract. fo. 285*b*; Fitz. *Nat. Brev.* 49; Bl. *Comm.* III, 252; Brunner, *Schwurgerichte* p. 324.

as of fee; if the infant has come to the land as heir of one who died seised as of fee, then the action against him must stand over until he is of full age. Now in this case the infant asserts that his ancestor died seised as of fee, and that therefore he need not answer; the demandant asserts that the infant's ancestor was not seised in fee, he was seised merely as guardian in chivalry. To settle this question a body of twelve men can be summoned. The question that they are to be asked is not the question formulated by the original writ, which concerns the alleged seisin of A's ancestor; it is quite another question relating to the alleged seisin of B's ancestor, and Glanvill is inclined to regard it as a 'prejudicial' question, that is to say an affirmative answer will not prove that A is entitled to recover, it will merely prove that B, albeit an infant, must answer A.[1] So again, to put another case, C may bring against D an action for land, claiming that he, C, mortgaged, or rather we must say 'gaged', the land to D for a sum of money which C now offers to pay; D, however, alleges that the land is his own, that he is seised in fee and not in gage; to decide this issue a body of recognitors is usually summoned, and if it declares that D holds in gage then D loses the land and loses the debt also, for he has chosen a particular mode of defence to the action, and has failed in it.[2] Glanvill seems half inclined to treat the questions that can thus be raised by pleading and answered by jury, as numerable and nameable; there is the recognition 'utrum quis sit infra aetatem an non', the recognition 'utrum de feodo vel de warda', the recognition 'utrum de feodo vel de vadio'; he even casually speaks of the body of recognitors thus called in to answer a question raised by pleading as an 'assisa'.[3] Our law we see might conceivably have taken this shape, that only certain particular issues, of which a list might be made, are to be decided by the new mode of trial, that in all other cases proof must be given in the old ways, by formal testimony, by compurgation, ordeal, battle. But really the questions which litigants can raise, which might well be decided by the oath of their neighbours, are innumerable. It becomes more and more a recognised principle that a defendant need not confine himself to a bare denial of the charge brought against him, that he may allege facts that disprove this charge, that if these facts be denied, the best way of deciding the dispute is to call in a set of twelve neighbours who will be likely to know and sworn to tell the truth. Such a body called in, not by the original writ, but in the course of the action, to determine a question of fact raised by the pleadings, gets the name of a jury (*jurata*) as contrasted with an assize (*assisa*); the

---

[1] Glanv. XIII, 14, 15.   [2] Glanv. XIII, 26–31.   [3] Glanv. XIII, 1, 2, 13, 31.

assisa is summoned by the 'original' writ issued out of the chancery before there has been any pleading; the *jurata* is summoned by a 'judicial' writ issuing out of the court before which the action is proceeding, and it comes to answer a question raised by the pleadings. Any considerable development of this principle, however, lies in the future; in Glanvill's book we see no more than this, that the practice of referring a disputed question to a body of 'recognitors' is beginning to extend itself outside the limits of the assizes.

We have now enumerated those actions begun by royal writ which were common in Glanvill's day. When from some seven years later (1194) we get the oldest roll of the king's court that has been preserved, we see that by far the greatest part—quite nine-tenths—of the litigation there recorded falls under the heads that we have already mentioned; Writs of Right, Assizes of Novel Disseisin, Mort d'Ancestor, and Darrein Presentment, these are common; other civil actions are rare. Still Glanvill knew some other civil actions. By attending to these for a while we may be able the better to understand the manner in which the king's justice grows, and the obstacles that impede its growth.

Claims for dower are not uncommon. According to the general principle which is now part of the law, the widow who wishes to bring an action for her dower must obtain a writ from the chancery; but according to the feudal principle the action should be begun in the court of him of whom the widow will hold her dower, that is to say, the court of her husband's heir, in the common case the court of her own son. We therefore find a Writ of Right of Dower, whereby the king commands the heir to hold full right to the widow concerning the hide of land which she claims to hold of him as her reasonable dower.[1] If the heir's court makes default then the action may be removed, like any other Writ of Right, to the county court, and thence it may be removed to the king's court. The appropriate mode of trial, if the widow's right be contested, is battle. But then we find this rule, which goes far to interfere with the feudal principle: If the woman has already got some part of her dower, then, as already said, her action must be begun in the feudal court, the heir's court; but if she has as yet got no part of her dower, then she must begin her action in the king's court. In order to do this she can obtain a Writ of Dower, *unde nihil habet*, which bids the sheriff to command the holder of the land to deliver to the widow her reasonable dower, 'whereof she complains that she has nothing' (*unde nihil habet ut dicit*), and in default of his so doing the sheriff is to

[1] Glanv. VI, 5.

summon him to the king's court, that he may state why he hath not done it.[1] Glanvill gives no explanation of this curious rule; but Bracton does, and the explanation is quite as curious as the rule. As the widow has not as yet got any part of her dower it is still possible that the holder of the land may deny the fact of the marriage. Now the fact of the marriage can only be proved by the bishop's certificate, marriage being a matter for the law ecclesiastic, and the only person who can compel the bishop to certify whether the woman was married or no is the king; to the mandate of the mere lord of a feudal court he would pay no heed. It follows that if there is any chance of a denial of the marriage the widow must go to the king's court.[2] Such is the pretext for the Writ of Dower *unde nihil habet*. Blackstone, looking at the matter from a modern point of view, turns the story topsy-turvy (*Comm.* III, 182, 183). It is an ingenious if rather flimsy excuse for allowing widows to sue in the king's court: Blackstone could hardly conceive that any such excuse could ever have been necessary. We have thus two forms of action concerning dower, and there is yet a third, namely the writ of Admeasurement of Dower, which lies when the widow has got more than she ought to have; this directs the sheriff to admeasure the land and allot to each party what is right.[3]

We turn to a matter of importance in social and economic history. There is a writ for the recovery of a serf, a 'nativus'. This writ, *de nativo habendo*, is directed to the sheriff, and bids him deliver to the claimant his fugitive bondman X, unless he has taken refuge on the royal demesne.[4] If, however, the person thus claimed asserts that he is free, and gives the sheriff security for the proof of his assertion, then the sheriff's power ceases, and the would-be free man obtains a writ *de libertate probanda*, which bids the sheriff put the case before the king's justices and summon the would-be lord to set forth his claim.[5] Why cannot this matter be tried in the county court? Glanvill gives no reason; Bracton says 'I can assign no reason unless it be in favour of liberty, which is a thing inestimable and not lightly to be trusted to the judgment of those who have but little skill.'[6] Whether then we prefer to suppose that we have here some relic of ancient times, of the time before feudalism, or to believe that Henry, who interfered in favour of the seisin of freehold, interfered also in favour of personal freedom, we have here a notable fact, the man who is claimed as a serf may go to the king's court and prove his liberty there.

[1] Glanv. VI, 15.   [2] Bract. fo. 106, 296*b*.   [3] Glanv. VI, 18; Bract. fo. 314.
[4] Glanv. XII, 11.   [5] Glanv. V, 2.   [6] Bract. fo. 105*b*.

As regards those claims which in after days give rise to the personal actions, those actions which, as we say, are founded on contract or founded on tort, Glanvill has but little to tell us; they are seldom prosecuted in the king's court. But the action of Debt is known there. As against the ecclesiastical courts the king has successfully asserted that actions for debt or for the detection of chattels, if they in no way concern marriage or testament and are brought against laymen, belong to the temporal not to the spiritual tribunals, and an action of Debt is occasionally brought in the king's own court.[1] The writ of Debt given by Glanvill[2] is of great interest for it seems to imply a very archaic conception. It is almost an exact copy of the *Praecipe in capite*, a certain sum of money being substituted for a certain piece of land. 'The king greets the sheriff. Command X that justly and without delay he render to A one hundred marks which he owes him, so he says, and of which he (A) complains that he (X) deforces him; and if he will not do so summon him by good summoners to be before me or my justices on such a day to show why he has not done it.' The non-payment of a debt seems regarded as a 'deforcement', an unjust and forcible detention of money that belongs to the creditor. We are tempted to say that Debt is a 'real' action, that the vast gulf which to our minds divides the 'Give me what I own' and 'Give me what I am owed' has not yet become apparent.[3] In this action of debt the old modes of proof still prevail; there may even be trial by battle as there may be in a Writ of Right and there is no mention of any jury, of anything comparable to the grand assize.[4]

In connexion with debts Glanvill speaks of mortgages of lands and of goods, or rather we must say of gages, for the term mortgage has at this time a very special sense. These gages occasionally give rise to actions in the royal court. There is already a writ for the gage creditor calling on the debtor to pay; there is another for the debtor calling on the gage creditor to receive his debt and give up the gaged land.[5] This latter writ is of interest, because it is the ancestor of a large family of writs. The commonest mode then in use of making land a security for the payment of money was to demise it to the creditor for a fixed term of years. The writ now in question is brought by the debtor who has made such a demise for a term that has expired, and who is now desirous of paying

---

[1] Glanv. X, 1. Observe the words 'si placitum illud ad curiam Regis trahere possit'.   [2] Glanv. X, 3.
[3] That there is a close connexion between the verbs *owe* and *own* is certain. Dr Skeat gives: 'Owe, to possess; hence to possess another's property, to be in debt, be obliged.'   [4] Glanv. X, 5.   [5] Glanv. X, 7, 9.

the debt and getting back the land: 'The king to the sheriff greeting. Command X that justly and without delay he render to A all the land in such a vill which he gaged to him for a sum of 100 marks for a term now past, as he says (*quam ei invadiavit pro centum marcis ad terminum qui praeteriit ut dicit*), and to receive his money, and if he will not do this summon him before our justices to show why he hath not done it.' Here we see is a *Praecipe* for land, but not a simple *Praecipe*; it is a *Praecipe* with a special reason assigned; A is not simply claiming the land as his own, he is claiming it as having been demised to X for a term that has expired; the writ assigns a reason why X should no longer hold the land; he has come to it by a title which no longer holds good. Now such writs for land, *Praecipes* with a reason assigned why the tenant's title is invalid, are going to play a great part in future history. The change of a few words would turn the writ now before us into one of the commonest of the 'Writs of Entry', the Writ of Entry *ad terminum qui praeteriit*. Here is the first germ of a great institution. We learn also that in this action, if the tenant affirms that he holds the land in fee, either party can have a 'recognition' to decide the question '*utrum ut feodum suum vel vadium suum*'. This is an important step; the action is not 'an assize'; the original writ says nothing about recognition, nothing about the mode of trial, but *either* party can, if he pleases, have twelve neighbours called in to answer the question 'fee or gage'. If neither cares for this new-fangled procedure then the case is treated as though it were one of Writ of Right, and there may be battle or grand assize to decide, not this narrow question, but the wider question whether A or X hath the greater right to this land.[1] We seem to catch the thought that when there has been some recent gage of the land easily provable by the testimony of the neighbours, it is hard on A that X should be allowed to raise the whole question of greater right, and force A to stake all on the issue of a battle. But still in this region of debt and gage, battle reigns as a normal mode of proof. Suppose that the creditor has a charter, a deed as we should say, if the debtor acknowledges the seal as his, well and good, he must pay even if he never put the seal there, for he ought to have taken better care of his seal; but if he denies that the impression on the wax is that of his seal, then there may be battle, though he may be debarred from this by a collation of the disputed document with other charters which admittedly bear his seal.[2] In another case relating to the loan of chattels Glanvill leaves us an unanswered query as to the mode of proof that is applicable, and makes no suggestion that the question should go to a jury.[3]

[1] Glanv. x, 9.   [2] Glanv. x, 12.   [3] Glanv. x, 13.

LECTURE IV

III. 1189–1272. This, our third period, extending from the death of Henry II to the accession of Edward I, is a period of rapid growth, as we learn from Bracton's treatise. New writs are freely invented, though towards the end of Henry III's reign this gives rise to murmurs and the barons seek to obtain a control over the king's writ-making power. There is now a large store of original writs which are writs of course (*brevia de cursu*), that is to say, they may be obtained from the subordinate officers of the royal chancery on payment of fees, the amount of which is becoming fixed. A Register of these writs of course has been formed and is kept in the chancery. The earliest Register known to me is one of 1227. In the Cambridge University Library we have two other Registers of Henry III's reign; Registers of Edward I's reign are common in MS. The size of the Register is rapidly increasing.

Litigation about land is still chiefly conducted by the proprietary action begun by writ of right, and the two possessory actions of Novel Disseisin and Mort d'Ancestor. When the tenement in question is held in chief of the Crown, instead of a writ of right there is a *Praecipe in capite*—but the lords have succeeded in getting a provision inserted in Magna Carta to the effect that such a writ as this, which at once summons the tenant before the king's court, shall not be used if the tenement is held of a mesne lord who has a court—in that case the action must be by writ of right (*breve de recto tenendo*) commanding the lord to do justice. But this victory of feudalism is illusive. Between the proprietary action and the possessory assizes there is growing up a large and popular group of *brevia de ingressu*—'Writs of Entry'. The characteristic of a writ of entry is that it orders the tenant to give up the land or answer the demandant's claim in the king's court—thus far following the form of the *Praecipe in capite*, but goes on to add that there is some specified and recent flaw in the tenant's title—he only had entry into the land, e.g. by the feoffment of a husband who was alienating his wife's inheritance, or by the feoffment of an infant, or by the feoffment of an abbot without consent of the monks, or by the feoffment of one who had disseised the demandant. This flaw, this recent flaw, in the tenant's title is suggested in order to take the case outside the rule that litigation about proprietary rights in land should be begun in the lord's court. The flaw must be recent. If the land has changed hands several times since the unlawful entry then no writ of entry is applicable and there must be a writ of right. The various writs of entry therefore are very numerous—there is one applicable to almost every conceivable case in which a tenant has come to the land by some title in which a recent flaw can be pointed out —we hear, for example, of a form of action as a writ of entry '*sur disseisin* in the *per*', a writ of entry '*sur disseisin* in the *per* and *cui*'.[1] In 1267 the Statute of Marlborough, which in many ways marks the end of feudalism, in effect abolished the restrictions on the formation of writs of entry—but it only did this by adding to their number. If since the unlawful entry the land had passed through several hands a writ of entry 'in the post' might be used—the demandant might allege that the tenant only had entry *post* (after) a disseisin committed by someone without showing how the land had passed from the disseisor to the tenant.

The words of the Statute (cap. 29) were as follows: 'Provisum est eciam, quod si alienaciones illae, de quibus breve de ingressu dari consuevit, per tot gradus fiant, quod breve illud in forma prius usitata haberi non possit, habeat conquerens breve de recuperanda seisina, sine mentiona graduum, ad cujuscunque manus per hujusmodi alienaciones res illa devenerit, per brevia originalia per consilium domini Regis providenda.'

'It is provided also, That if those alienations (whereupon a writ of entry was wont to be granted) hap to be made in so many degrees, that by reason thereof the same writ cannot be made in the form beforetime used, the plaintiffs shall have a writ to recover their seisin, without making mention of the degrees, into whose hands soever the same thing shall happen to come by such alienations, and that by an original writ to be provided therefor by the council of our lord the King.'[2]

We are accustomed to regard the English real actions as a hopeless tangle—this is the result of the writs of entry. If we place ourselves at the death of Henry II the situation is really very simple. Let us review the position. If a proprietary action is to be brought for land it must be begun by *Praecipe quod reddat* (after Magna Carta, 1215, this is only permissible where the demandant claims to hold in chief of *Dominus Rex*) or by *Breve de recto tenendo*. In either case the demandant will have to allege that the land is *jus et haereditatem suam*—will have, i.e. to rely upon proprietary right. He will have a proprietary, petitory, droiturel action, in the language of the Roman Law a *vindicatio rei*. Besides this there are two possessory actions, each of narrow scope and analogous to

---

[1] For the form of these writs of entry see the Select Writs, below.
[2] This is the translation given in the Statutes at Large.

the possessory interdicts: (1) The Novel Disseisin, which is the English counterpart of the Roman Interdict *Unde Vi* and is probably derived from that source immediately through the *actio spolii* of the Canon Law. It has a narrow limit; A complains that X has disseised him—that this very X has ousted this very A from seisin. If that be so then, without any discussion of 'right', A ought to be put back into seisin—'*salvo jure cujuslibet*'. (2) The Mort d'Ancestor: B has died seised as of fee—not necessarily 'as of right'—he had, or behaved as having, heritable rights, A is his next heir, but, before A could enter, X entered. If this be so, X is to be turned out of seisin and A placed in seisin of that land. As I understand there was a good Roman analogy for this too, the *haereditatis petitio possessoria*, but it is doubtful whether this was known to the lawyers of Henry II.

These possessory assizes are marked off from the proprietary action, first by a summary royal procedure, in which essoins are reduced to a minimum, and secondly by their short periods of limitation.

Then come the writs of entry invented in the time of Richard, John, and Henry III. A writ of entry is, as we have seen, a writ of *praecipe* suggesting a recent flaw of a particular kind in the tenant's title. Their object seems to have been to evade feudal jurisdiction, probably on the theory that they are in a certain sense possessory and therefore do not fall to the lords. The demandant relies on a recent seisin, hence these writs are confined within 'the degrees', that is to say they are competent only if the tenant is first, second or third faulty possessor.[1] Even this limit is removed by the Statute of Marlborough after which a writ of entry can be used if it can be said that the tenant came to the land after some faulty or wrongful entry.

It is these writs which make the history of our forms of action so very complex and unintelligible. Are they proprietary, are they possessory? The answer seems to be that in their working they are proprietary, in their origin possessory or quasi-possessory, since the justification for litigation in the king's court lies in the notion that the demandant has recent seisin on his side.

---

[1] Here Professor Maitland has in mind the writs of entry *sur disseisin* or on intrusion; in other instances, 'the degrees' stretched only to the second faulty possessor, e.g. where the tenant C is alleged to have entered *per* B *cui* A the husband (*cui invita*) or the idiot (*dum con compos*) or the doweress or life tenant (*ad communem legem* etc.). In these cases A cannot be said to be a faulty possessor, in that of the idiot or infant he may even be the demandant himself —it would perhaps be more accurate in the text to say 'if the tenant is first, second or third from the creator of the flaw in the title'.

The result of this, as to substantive law, is that we seem to get a *tertium quid* between property and possession, between *jus* and *seisina*. To this I shall recur.[1]

In what I have just said I have been compelled to contradict Blackstone. He treats the writs of entry as older than the assizes. 'In the times of our Saxon ancestors, the right of possession seems only to have been recoverable by writ of entry.'[2] 'Thus Henry II probably in the twenty-second year of his reign gave the assizes of novel disseisin and mort d'ancestor.' In this last statement there is I think a small mistake. Blackstone refers these two assizes to the Council held at Northampton in 1176. Now it is very possible that the Mort d'Ancestor was created on that occasion, and that we have the words which created it in an instruction to the itinerant justices, some words of which Bracton cites in a note and the whole of which will be found in the Select Charters. But the Novel Disseisin seems about ten years older—we have not got the text of the ordinance which created it, but on the Pipe Roll for 12 Henry II we begin to have entries of fines inflicted *pro disseisina super assisam Regis*. There can I think be little doubt that the ordinance was made at the Council of Clarendon in 1166. But this mistake is small compared with that of supposing that the writs of entry are older than the assizes, and I need hardly say that it is nonsense to suppose that our Saxon ancestors knew anything about writs of entry. As to their date, we must start with the fact that Glanvill gives no writ of entry, though (x, 9) he has got just one writ which might easily be converted into a writ of entry *ad terminum qui praeteriit*. The Registers of the early years of Henry III give two such writs, the writ of entry *ad terminum qui praeteriit* and the writ *cui in vita*, and on a Patent Roll of 1205, there is a writ of entry *sur disseisin*, a writ for the disseisee against the heir of the disseisor, followed by a writ which directs that this henceforward shall be a writ of course (Rot. Pat. i. 32); before the middle of the century we find almost all the writs of entry in use, except those which were afterwards given by statute. The truth is that the writs of entry presuppose the assizes. Suppose that X has disseised A and that X is still in seisin, there is no writ of entry applicable to this simple case, because it is a case for an Assize of Novel Disseisin. If X dies and his heir Y enters then there is a writ of entry for A against Y, because there cannot be an assize, for an Assize of Novel Disseisin can only be brought against a disseisor. It is true that very late in the day we do find a writ of entry covering the ground of the Assize of Novel Disseisin, 'the writ of entry

---

[1] Below, p. 37.   [2] *Comm.* III, 184.

in the nature of an assize'; but I do not believe that this writ appears until very late times, until Richard II's reign, when the procedure by way of assize has become more clumsy than the procedure by writ of entry —more clumsy because more antiquated. I have been compelled to insist on this point, because Blackstone's theory turns the whole history of seisin upside down.

Meanwhile a number of other gaps are being filled up with new writs. For instance, the Assize of Mort d'Ancestor, as we have seen,[1] lies only when the claimant can assert that the person who has just died in seisin, and whose heir he is, was his father, mother, sister, brother, uncle, aunt. It had been sufficient to provide for the common cases; if the dead person was the claimant's grandfather or cousin the assize could not be used. This gap was filled up in 1237 by the action of Aiel, Besaiel and Cosinage, though the lords resisted these new inventions. So again the group of writs relating to advowsons has received additions, and there is another group relating to wardships and marriages. Here again we see the line between proprietary and possessory actions; besides the proprietary writ of right of ward there is the possessory action of ejectment of ward.

There are also writs for settling disputes between lord and tenant— writs relating to easements, writs relating to rights of common. Very frequently there is one writ which is deemed possessory and one which is deemed proprietary or droiturel—thus there is an assize of nuisance and a writ *quod permittat prosternere* for the abatement of nuisances which cannot be brought within the terms of the assize. The group of actions relating to land and to the so-called incorporeal hereditaments is a very large one—but the forms which hereafter will deserve attention are the possessory assizes, the writs of entry, and the writ of right. They form a sort of hierarchy of actions—the writs of entry seem to bridge the gulf between possession and property, between seisin and right. This, as we shall hereafter see, is a very remarkable feature of English Law.

An illustration of the important results of the invention of new writs may be found in the remedies granted to termors. Slowly a practice has arisen of letting land for terms of years. At first the termor's right is regarded as a merely contractual right—his only remedy is an action of covenant against his lessor—indeed in the first half of the thirteenth century we seldom find the action of covenant used for any other purpose. If ejected by his lessor, the termor can recover the land by action of covenant; if disturbed or ejected by anyone else his one

---

[1] Above, p. 25.

remedy is to obtain by the same action damages from the lessor who has contracted that he shall enjoy the land during the term. He is not regarded as having any right in the land, or any seisin, i.e. possession, of the land, he has only, as we should say, *jus in personam*. But about 1237, as it would seem, a new writ was given him, the *quare ejecit infra terminum* which would enable him to recover the land from any person who ejected him, at least if that person claimed under the lessor. Bracton thought that it would enable him to recover against any ejector; but the form which came into use supposed that the defendant was a purchaser from the lessor, and it seems to have been held that it could not be brought against a mere stranger to the title. We are even told who invented this writ; it was William Raleigh, the chief justice. There is no legislation, no intention to give a new right, merely a new remedy; but as you see the character of the old right is being changed, it is ceasing to be a merely contractual *jus in personam*. In a few years we have Bracton discussing the problem whether the termor is not seised of the land. Undoubtedly his lessor is seised, and if the termor be ejected by a third person the lord can recover the land from that third person as from one who has disseised him;—but the termor also is getting protection—what are we to say, can two persons at one and the same time be seised or possessed of the same acre in two different rights? Bracton hesitates—Roman law points one way, English practice another. In course of time in the fifteenth century there will be a differentiation of terms, the termor will be possessed, the freeholder will at the same time be seised. Our law thus has on its hands the very difficult task of working two different sets of possessory remedies—the ancient set which protect seisin, the more modern set which protect possession. Then 'seised' will come to imply the right to use the assizes competent to the freeholder, 'possessed' will imply the right to use the writ of trespass.

Meanwhile the actions which came to be known as personal make their appearance. The oldest seems to be 'Debt-Detinue', which appears already in Glanvill. I say 'Debt-Detinue'—originally men see little distinction between the demand for a specific chattel and the demand for a certain sum of money. Gradually this action divides itself into two, Detinue for a specific chattel, Debt for a sum of money—this differentiation takes place early in the thirteenth century. As in Detinue the judgment given for the plaintiff awards him either the chattel itself, or its value; and, as the defendant thus has the option of giving back the chattel or paying its value, Bracton is led to make the important remark that there is no real action for chattels—an important remark, for it is the foundation of all our talk about real and personal property. To Debt and Detinue we must now add Replevin, the action for goods unlawfully taken in distress. This action we are told was invented in John's reign— another tradition ascribed its invention to Glanvill. Covenant also has appeared, though during the first half of the thirteenth century it is seldom used except in cases of what we should call leases of land for terms of years. Gradually the judges came to the opinion that the only acceptable evidence of a covenant is a sealed writing, and one of the foundations of our law of contract is thus laid. Account appears in Henry III's reign; but it is very rare and seems only used against bailiffs of manors.

But the most important phenomenon is the appearance of Trespass— that fertile mother of actions. Instances of what we cannot but call actions of trespass are found even in John's reign, but I think it clear that the writ of trespass did not become a writ of course until very late in Henry III's reign. Now trespass is to start with a semi-criminal action. It has its roots in criminal law, and criminal procedure. The historical importance of trespass is so great that we may step aside to look at the criminal procedure out of which it grew. The old criminal action (yes, action) was the Appeal of Felony (*appellum de felonia*). It was but slowly supplanted by indictment—the procedure of the common accuser set going by Henry II, the appeal on the other hand being an action brought by a person aggrieved by the crime. The appellant had to pronounce certain accusing words.[1] In each case he must say of the appellee '*fecit hoc* (the murder, rape, robbery or mayhem) *nequiter et in felonia, vi et armis et contra pacem Domini Regis*'.

He charges him with a wicked deed of violence to be punished by death, or in the twelfth century by mutilation. The procedure is stringent with outlawry in default of appearance. The new phenomenon appears about the year 1250, it is an action which might be called an attenuated appeal based on an act of violence. The defendant is charged with a breach of the king's peace, though with one that does not amount to felony. Remember that throughout the Middle Ages there is no such word as misdemeanour—the crimes which do not amount to felony are

---

[1] See, for example, Bracton, fo. 138*a*, for the accusation by a brother in an appeal of murder (reciting that the appellor and his brother, the murdered man, were in the peace of God and of our Lord the King at such a place and on such a day) where the words '*vi et armis*' do not appear but are replaced by setting out the detail of the assault and the mortal wounding with a sword.

trespasses (Lat. *transgressiones*). The action of trespass is founded on a breach of the king's peace: with force and arms the defendant has assaulted and beaten the plaintiff, broken the plaintiff's close, or carried off the plaintiff's goods; he is sued for damages. The plaintiff seeks not violence but compensation, but the unsuccessful defendant will also be punished and pretty severely. In other actions the unsuccessful party has to pay an amercement for making an unjust, or resisting a just claim; the defendant found guilty of trespass is fined and imprisoned. What is more, the action for trespass shows its semi-criminal nature in the process that can be used against a defendant who will not appear—if he will not appear, his body can be seized and imprisoned; if he cannot be found, he may be outlawed. We thus can see that the action of trespass is one that will become very popular with plaintiffs because of the stringent process against defendants. I very much doubt whether in Henry III's day the action could as yet be used save where there really had been what we might fairly call violence and breach of the peace; but gradually the convenience of this new action showed itself. In order to constitute a case for 'Trespass *vi et armis*', it was to the last necessary that there should be some wrongful application of physical force to the defendant's lands or goods or person—but a wrongful step on his land, a wrongful touch to his person or chattels was held to be force enough and an adequate breach of the king's peace. This action then has the future before it.

Meanwhile trial by jury is becoming the normal mode of trying disputed questions of fact. The older modes of trial are falling into the background. In Debt and Detinue and some other cases there still is compurgation. The obsolescence of this ancient mode of proof, however, is a gradual process. It cannot be explained by rationalistic statements such as that in Debt and Detinue the cause of action is one peculiarly within the knowledge of the defendant. We must look rather to the historical order of development of the various actions. Debt and Detinue are formulated at an early period; Trespass is the product of a later age. But the permissibility of this old mode of proof in Debt and Detinue is of great importance—it sets men on attempting to substitute for them, even within their own sphere, forms of action in which there will be trial by jury. And so with the forms of trial appropriate to the assizes. Though in a large sense this may be called a sub-form of trial by jury, still it is an archaic sub-form and men try to evade it; they would gladly, if they could, use actions of trespass instead of the novel disseisin, and the mort d'ancestor. In these old assizes the question for the recognitors was formulated in the original writ; in the newer forms the procedure was more flexible—a jury was only called in after the parties to the action had by their pleadings come to some issue of fact—it was not called in until pleading had decided what exactly was the real point of dispute.

IV. 1272–1307. The reign of 'the English Justinian' may be treated as a period by itself—a period of statutory activity. Statutes made by king and parliament now interfere with many details both of substantive law and of procedure. A number of new actions are given by statute, e.g. the De Donis gives the issue in tail the 'formedon in the descender'; this is a well-known and typical example. The whole system stiffens. Men have learnt that a power to invent new remedies is a power to create new rights and duties, and it is no longer to be suffered that the chancellor or the judges should wield this power. How far the process of crystallisation had gone, how rigid the system was becoming, we learn from a section of the Statute of Westminster II, 13 Edw. I c. 24 (1285). Men have been obliged to depart from the Chancery without getting writs, because there are none which will exactly fit their cases, although these cases fall within admitted principles. It is not to be so for the future—'Et quotienscumque de cetero evenerit in Cancellaria quod in uno casu reperitur breve et in consimili casu cadente sub eodem jure et simili indigente remedio, concordent clerici de Cancellaria in brevi faciendo vel atterminent querentes in proximo parliamento et scribant casus in quibus concordare non possunt et referant eos ad proximum parliamentum et de consensu jurisperitorum fiat breve ne contingat de cetero quod curia diu deficiat querentibus in justicia perquirenda.' 'And whensoever from henceforth it shall fortune in the Chancery, that in one case a writ is found, and in like case falling under like law, and requiring like remedy, is found none, the clerks of the Chancery shall agree in making the writ; or adjourn the plaintiffs until the next Parliament, and let the cases be written in which they cannot agree, and let them refer them until the next Parliament, and by consent of men learned in the law, a writ shall be made, lest it might happen after that the court should long time fail to minister justice unto complainants.' In after times we hear complaints that the Chancery made but little use of the permission thus given to it; but for my own part I doubt whether it enjoyed or was intended to enjoy any very considerable liberty. It may vary the old writs—but it is not to invent new rights or new remedies—*in consimili casu cadente sub eodem jure et simili indigente remedio*. But when we say that but little use was made of this Statute there is one great exception. It is regarded as the statutory warrant for the variation of the writs of trespass so as to suit special cases, until at length—about the end of the Middle Ages—lawyers perceive that they have a new form 'Trespass upon the special case' or 'Case'. Specialised forms of this branch off forming (1) Assumpsit, so important in the law of Contract, (2) Trover, (3) Deceit, (4) Action upon the Case for words —slander and libel. It is worth noting that a writ issued by the Chancery is not necessarily a good writ. The justices may quash it as contrary to law, and in the later Middle Ages the judges are conservative; they hold the writ bad not merely if it does not suit the case but if it contravenes what they deem legal principle. At any rate the tale of common law (i.e. non-statutory) actions was now regarded as complete.[1] The king's courts had come to be regarded as omnicompetent courts, they had to do all the important civil justice of the realm and to do it with the limited supply of forms of action which had been gradually accumulated in the days when feudal justice and ecclesiastical justice were serious competitors with royal justice.

---

[1] *Notandum.* Registrum Brevium—printed by Rastell 1531, Medieval Register MS. (there are many in the University Library). The earliest seen by me is a Register sent by Henry to Ireland—it contains about fifty writs. There is an early Register of Henry III in the University Library (ii. 6. 13). This book has grown to perhaps fifty times its bulk when printed under Hen. VIII; there is the work of four centuries in it. There are Commentaries; the Old Natura Brevium and Fitzherbert's Natura Brevium published 1534 (Fitz. ob. 1538). His work which Coke called 'an exact work exquisitely penned' ran through many editions. The theme of the expounder is not the nature of rights but the nature of writs.

LECTURE V

V. 1307–1833. A period lasting from 1307 to 1833 is enormously long, still I do not know that for our present purpose it could be well broken up into sub-periods. Our interest must be chiefly concentrated on the action of trespass. We may perhaps draw a map of the ground. Here is a sketch (see next page).

I have tried to assign dates in a rough way to the various developments of trespass; but you should understand that this, from the nature of the case, must be a somewhat arbitrary proceeding. So continuous is legal history that the lawyers do not see that there has been a new departure until this has for some time past been an accomplished fact; their technical terminology will but slowly admit the fact that a single form of action has become several forms of action.

From Edward I's day onwards trespass *vi et armis* is a common action. We may notice three main varieties—unlawful force has been used against the body, the goods, the land of the plaintiff; so we have trespass in assault and battery, trespass *de bonis asportatis*, trespass *quare clausum fregit*. These are the main varieties, but the writ can be varied to meet other cases and sometimes states the facts of the particular case pretty fully, e.g. the defendant has not only assaulted the plaintiff, but has imprisoned him and kept him in prison so many days, or again, the defendant's dog has bitten the plaintiff's sheep. But for a while it seems essential that there should be some unlawful force, however slight, something that can by a stretch of language be called a breach of the peace. Now, among other things that the writ of trespass can do is that it can protect possession of land. If B trespasses on the land which A possesses, A can recover damages from B by a writ of trespass *quare vi et armis*—B has broken A's close and the king's peace. A can recover damages, but if B proceeds to eject A, though A may recover damages he cannot recover possession of the land by this writ. If A wants to recover possession he must bring an assize or a writ of entry, or a writ of right. Now the possession which is thus protected by the *quare vi et armis* is something different from the seisin which is protected by the assizes. The action of trespass grows up in an age in which the letting of land for terms of years has become a common practice—and if land be so let to a farmer and a stranger trespass, it is the termor, not the free-holder, who will be able to complain that the stranger has entered and broken his close. Indeed, after some little hesitation, it is admitted that if the lessor without justification enters the land demised to the termor, the termor will be able to bring a writ of trespass against him, albeit the lessor has only entered on land of which he himself is seised. Thus we

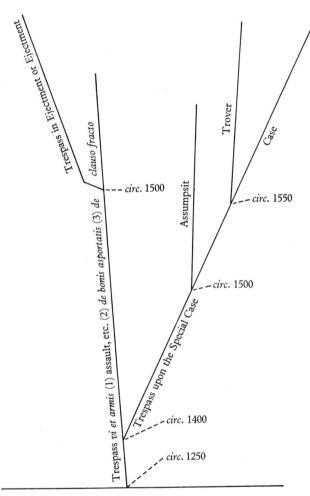

Criminal Procedure

are coming to have two protected possessions, the old possession or seisin protected by the assizes, the new possession protected by the writ of trespass. The two terms become specified. We may, I think, fix upon the middle of the fifteenth century as the time of the specification.

Littleton, who wrote between 1474 and 1481, in section 324 says in effect that a termor is not seised but is possessed. But in section 567 he himself slips into speaking of the termor as seised.

So again, the holder in villeinage now gets protection. The assizes did not protect him; they did not protect him against mere strangers, much less against his lord. The assize of novel disseisin required that the plaintiff should be disseised *de libero tenemento suo*. To have extended the royal protection to holders in villeinage would have been too bold a measure even for Henry II. The view of the king's court was that the lord of the manor was seised of the villein tenements. If a stranger ejects one of the villein tenants it is the lord not the tenant who is disseised. The tenant's remedy was an action in the lord's court, and so long as the manorial courts were efficient tribunals the tenant in villeinage, even though personally a villein, was, I think, very fairly and efficiently protected against all but his lord. Times had changed when the action of trespass became common at the end of the thirteenth century. The new action was based on violence and breach of the peace. The mere tenant at will was allowed that action, was allowed to call the land *clausum suum*. Putting the rights of the tenant in villeinage at their lowest, he was still a tenant at will, and as such should have the action of trespass against all but the lord. Then in the middle of the fifteenth century we begin to hear hints that he may bring trespass even against his lord. In 1457 we hear such a hint; and in 1467 and 1481 it is definitely said that the copyholder—that is the new name for the tenant in villeinage, shall have an action against the lord if ejected contrary to the custom of the manor. This, of course, is an enormously important step.

Thus there are many persons protected in possession by the writ of trespass who are not seised. But the protection thus given is only that of an action for damages—one cannot recover possession by means of such an action. However, just at the end of the Middle Ages there comes a change. The special form of a writ of trespass applicable to the case of an ejected lessee is known as a writ *de ejectione firmae*, it calls on the defendant to answer 'quare vi et armis intravit [unum mesuagium] quod M demisit praedicto A ad terminum qui nondum praeteriit et ipsum A ejecit de praedicta firma sua ... contra pacem nostram'. It is just a writ of trespass *vi et armis*. Now, at the very end of the fourteenth century it seems perfectly settled that this writ will only give damages and will not restore the plaintiff to the land (Pasch. 6 Ric. II, Fitz. Abr. *Ejectione firmae*, pl. 2). On the other hand, about the middle of the fifteenth century, lawyers certainly speak as though possession might be recovered by this writ (Pasch. 7 Edw. IV (1467), fo. 6, pl. 16; Mich. 21 Edw. IV (1481), fo. 11, pl. 2). A judgment of 14 Hen. VII, in error, however, seems to have been necessary to decide the point finally (Fitz. N. B. 220, 1491–2). Thus it became settled that judgment might be given that the plaintiff do recover his term, and a writ might go to the sheriff bidding him put the plaintiff in possession—*habere facias possessionem*. This step may have been easier because there was an older writ—*quare ejecit infra terminum*—whereby a termor might recover possession from persons claiming under the lessor.

To sum up for a moment. Early in the reign of Henry III the termor's remedy was an action of covenant.[1]

Raleigh invented the writ of *quare ejecit infra terminum*. Bracton thought it would enable the termor to recover *contra quoscunque dejectores*.[2] However (and this is a good instance of inflexibility) the writ actually settled supposed the ejector to have bought from the lessor. It was then held that the writ only lies against those claiming under the lessor.

Then Trespass comes into use—and one specialised form of trespass *quare vi et armis*, is trespass *de ejectione firmae*—this lies against all, but only for damages.

[Fitzherbert (N. B. 198 A) begins a confusion which has misled later writers. He supposes *ejectione firmae* to be older than *quare ejecit infra terminum*—which is not true. He also supposes trespass primeval—this certainly is not true.]

The action of trespass *de ejectione firmae* becomes the Action of Ejectment, and the common means of recovering possession of land, no matter the kind of title that the claimant asserts. What makes this action of ejectment so interesting is the process whereby the freeholder acquires the termor's remedy. Why did he want it? The reasons are twofold, first the dilatoriness of the old proprietary or droiturel action with their essoins, vouchers, and possible trial by battle or the grand assize, and secondly the rudeness of the old possessory actions, each with its narrow formula (a process which confines the jurors to the answering of questions of pure fact, a process carried out under cover of a highly technical system of pleading which sets many traps for the litigant). But this step is only made under cover of an elaborate fiction. It may occur to you to ask why so elaborate a fiction is necessary. Has not the principle been conceded that possession may be recovered in an

---

[1] Bracton, fo. 220, and Cambridge Register, *circ.* 1237.
[2] Bracton, fo. 220.

action for trespass? A claims land against X, why should he be compelled to say that he, A, demised the land to John Doe, who was ejected,
and bring the action in John Doe's name—why should it not be enough,
in an action of trespass, to say that A himself was ejected? The answer
to that is I think this—if you are a freeholder claiming land you should
bring a writ of entry, or a writ of right. If you, being freeholder, have
been ejected, that is a disseisin, you should bring the assize of novel disseisin. The law has provided you with abundant remedies, both proprietary and possessory—you must use them. If to us it seems that such
an answer as this is unsatisfactory we should try to look at the matter
from X's point of view. Has he not, so to speak, a vested interest in the
maintenance of the old procedure. You are proposing to use against him
an action in which he may be imprisoned and outlawed, while, supposing that he is in the wrong, the law has provided other forms of action
which do not permit this procedure against his person. Arguments of
this kind have had a considerable influence on the course of our legal
history, and have produced very odd results—a newer, and perhaps less
common right, is sanctioned by a modern and comparatively rapid action, while older, and perhaps commoner, rights are protected only by
old and clumsy remedies.

However, in the present case, as is well known, a dodge was discovered by which the action of ejectment (*ejectione firmae*) could be
made generally available as a means of enabling any claimant to recover
possession of land. Blackstone has described this dodge fully and well.[1]
You are in possession of land of which I say that I am the true owner,
the tenant in fee simple. If this is correct I have as a general rule a right
to enter. Mark, 'as a general rule'; for there are exceptions—the cases
where the entry is 'tolled', of which hereafter.[2] I do in fact enter and
then and there make a lease for years to a third person, John Doe. John
Doe stays on the land until ousted by you, and then brings the action,
trespass in ejectment or, briefly, ejectment. To succeed in his action he
must prove (1) my *right to enter*, (2) the *lease*, (3) his *entry* under the
lease and (4) his *ouster* by you. When all this is proved he recovers his
term with damages. Upon this form there is a variation. I put John Doe
as tenant upon the land and he is ousted not by you but by a fourth
person, William Stiles. Doe then has the action of ejectment against
Stiles, but there is a rule that no plaintiff shall proceed in ejectment
without notice being given to the person actually in possession and an
opportunity being given him to appear as a defendant if he pleases.

[1] *Comm.* III, 201.   [2] Below, p. 49.

Where Doe sues Stiles, Stiles informs you of the action and you, if you do not want to see the land adjudged to Doe, defend the action in Stiles's stead. In the end my title as against you is put in issue in the action.

Then the Court in effect says 'Here is an action in which any title can be tried. Why not abbreviate the process by supposing that things have been done which in fact have not been done?' The ultimate outcome is that, bringing my action in the name of Doe (for on the record I am merely the 'lessor of the plaintiff'), I tell of (1) a lease to Doe, (2) an entry and (3) an ouster by Stiles, the 'casual ejector'. I then send you a notice purporting to be signed by 'your loving friend, William Stiles' to the effect that he claims no interest but advises you to defend; and the Court will only allow you to defend in place of Stiles the action that I bring in the name of Doe if you will agree to confess at the trial the *lease*, *entry* and *ouster* and leave the trial to go upon the merits of the title only.

The development of this action is a long story and about such a matter it is hard to fix any dates—one cannot tell the exact moment at which a proceeding becomes fictitious—but I believe we may say that during the Tudor reigns the action of ejectment became the regular mode of recovering the possession of land. A few improvements remained to be invented under the Stuarts, and the perfection of the action is attributed to the Lord Chief Justice Rolle of the Upper Bench during the Commonwealth; but already in the day of James I Coke expressed his deep regret that the assizes and real actions were going out of use. That is in the Preface to 8 Rep., in which book Coke reports two assizes of Novel Disseisin, one writ of dower and a formedon in the remainder. Blackstone still says that 'the plaintiff ought to be some real person, and not merely an ideal fictitious one who hath no existence, as is frequently though unwarrantably practised'.[1]

It is worth while to notice the form taken by the title of the action. The action which would today be known as *Atkyns* v. *Horde* was entitled *Doe on the demise of Atkyns* v. *Horde* or, briefly, *Doe dem. Atkyns* v. *Horde*, Atkyns appearing as the 'lessor of the plaintiff'.

The real actions never went quite out of use until they were abolished by statute in 1833 and a few were brought in the nineteenth century. There were to the last certain cases—possible rather than probable—in which a man was entitled to the possession of land but could not bring an action of ejectment for it. The basis of the action of ejectment was the right of the 'lessor of the plaintiff' to enter upon the land. The

---

[1] *Comm.* III, 203.

action presupposes that the plaintiff has not merely a better right than the defendant but a right to enter on the defendant and it was possible that a man had the former and not the latter.

To understand these exceptional cases we must go back to the strict possessory protection of seisin to the days when, at all costs, force was forbidden. An ejector must be re-ejected at once or never, in Bracton's time, *infra quatuor dies*. The Roman owner turned out by armed force may only repossess himself by armed force there and then—*non ex intervallo sed ex continenti*—otherwise he must have recourse to the *interdict unde vi*.[1] In the later Middle Ages, however, this strict possessory protection was gradually relaxed in favour of a doctrine that the man with the better right (the true owner) generally has a right to enter. The older rule becomes a string of exceptions to the newer rule. Certain events are said to 'toll' (i.e. to take away) the entry of the true owner—to leave him with a right only to bring an action, a writ of entry. The story is a very difficult one to explain here and one which is hardly for beginners. For example it may however be said that (1) a descent cast to an heir tolls entry and (2) a discontinuance (in particular, a tortious feoffment in fee simple) turns a right of entry into a right of action. So, then, to the end there were some exceptions to what had become the general rule that title to land could be made good in Ejectment.

I have said 'to the end', that is to say until 1833. As we have seen[2] the action of ejectment, with all its fictions, was spared from the wholesale abolition of real and mixed actions made by the Real Property Limitation Act of 1833, and it was reformed by the Common Law Procedure Act of 1852.[3] The fictitious procedure was abolished, the real claimant was to sue in his own name, John Doe disappeared. The action thus remodelled was in use until 1875. Since that time we have had in the old sense no forms of action—an action for the recovery of land, an action, i.e. to obtain possession of land, can be brought by any person entitled to possession, no matter the nature of his title, be it freehold, leasehold, copyhold.

Let us recall the accepted definition of the words 'real', 'personal', and 'mixed' as applied to actions; meaning, that is to say, actions of which the result is the recovery of the thing or of damages or of both, respectively: and let us examine in somewhat greater detail into the personal actions.

We may say that they were nine in number, (1) Replevin, (2) Detinue,

---

[1] Dig. 43, 16, 3, 9.   [2] Above, p. 6.

[3] 15 and 16 Vic. c. 76, sec. 168 ff.

(3) Debt, (4) Account, (5) Covenant, (6) Trespass, (7) Case, (8) Trover, and (9) Assumpsit.

Replevin we may quickly put aside, its importance in the Middle Ages was very great, but it was not capable of much development. It is an action founded upon a wrongful distraint—the distrainee offers security that he will contest the distrainor's rights in court, and thereupon the distrainor is bound to surrender the goods—usually cattle. If he does not do so the sheriff is to raise the *posse comitatus* and retake them. An action beginning thus with a demand for replevin (i.e. that the goods be 'repledged' pending action) becomes the normal mode of trying the rightfulness of distraint, and such actions are of very common occurrence in the Middle Ages.

A procedure for securing the delivery of goods by way of replevin still exists—the registrar of the County Court playing the old part of the sheriff. A few instances of replevin used to recover goods though not taken by way of distress are known. These occur late in the day, and are not important in relation to general theory.

Detinue.[1] This is a very old action. The defendant is charged with an unjust detainer (not, be it noted, an unjust taking)—*injuste detinet*. This action looks very like a real action. The writ originating it bears a close similarity with the writ of right (*praecipe in capite*), but in the first place the mesne process is not *in rem*, and in the second (and this is very important) the defendant when worsted is always allowed the option of surrendering the goods or paying assessed damages. The reason of this may perhaps be found partly in the perishable character of medieval moveables, and the consequent feeling that the court could not accept the task of restoring them to their owners, and partly in the idea that all things had a 'legal price' which, if the plaintiff gets, is enough for him.

This option leads Bracton to say that there is no real action for chattels, and this sentence is the starting-point of the fashion which teaches us to say that goods and chattels are not 'real' but 'personal' property.

Behind all this probably lies the time when the doctrine is current that *mobilia non habent sequelam*, which doctrine, though never in the mouth of English lawyers, runs through French law down to modern times. If I let my goods go out of my possession with my will and consent I am to have no action against any third hand—a bailee of my bailee, or even a taker from my bailee. When I put my trust in the promise of my bailee I have that promise in exchange for my ownership,

---

[1] See also above, p. 38.

as the German proverb has it, 'where one has put his trust there must he seek it again'. But the English law never reached a full conformity with this theory. Modern English law is, on the other hand, highly favourable to owners of chattels. Subject to the ancient exception about sales in market overt, and to modern statutory exceptions (now embodied in the Factors Act, 1889, and the Sale of Goods Act, 1893), ownership is never lost by acts of others than the owner. But this is clearly not the starting-point—of old the property in moveables is not so intense as property in land; and archaic law finds difficulty in giving two rights in the one thing, one to the owner and another to his bailee. At any rate, however this may be, the terminology became fixed—there is no 'real' action for moveables, and therefore chattels are not 'real property'.

Here we must note the great defect of the action for Detinue—a defect which it shares with its sister Debt—the defendant may wage and make his law, in other words, may resort to the compurgatory oath. Attempts have been made to rationalise and explain this fact. It has been said that debt and detinue were matters more particularly within the knowledge of the parties, and so on, but the simple explanation is that detinue and debt were older than trial by jury.[1] But wager of law was abolished in 1833 by 3 and 4 Will. IV, c. 42, sec. 13.

Debt.[2] An action for a fixed sum of money due for any reason, and own sister to Detinue. Here also we have a *praecipe quod reddat*. *Praecipe quod reddat* (1) *terram*, (2) *catalla*, (3) *pecunia* are the writs of right (for land), of detinue, and of debt respectively.

Its first and chief use was for the recovery of money lent—a sense in which the word 'recovery' is still used. The difference between *commodatum* and *mutuum*—the loan to be returned and the loan to be repaid—was hardly seen. It is hardly seen today by the vulgar. 'My money at the bank', is a phrase in common use. Another use of the action of debt was for the recovery of the price upon a sale, and another the recovery of rent due. There were other *causae debendi*, and gradually the progress towards generalization got to be expressed in the phrase that debt would lie for a fixed sum of money if there were a *quid pro quo* or, later, if there were 'consideration'. Thus Debt, originally conceived as recuperatory, like Detinue, becomes capable of being used for the enforcement of contracts of sorts. One limitation, however, remained— the untranscendible limit—the claim must be for a fixed sum. Debt cannot be used to obtain compensation for breach of contract. And, further,

---

[1] They appear in very early registers.
[2] See also above, pp. 31 and 38.

debt can always be met by wager of law, which becomes more and more absurd. It is never forgotten that the action of debt is not necessarily based on contract—it serves for the recovery of statutory penalties, of forfeitures under by-laws, of amercements, and of monies adjudged by a court to be due.

Account. The action of Account is another *praecipe*, originally granted against manorial bailiffs. *Praecipe quod reddat compotum.* Auditors were appointed to supervise the account. At a later stage it was extended to some other classes, thus it could be used between partners, but partnership is uncommon and unimportant in the England of the Middle Ages. A few modern instances of its use are recorded, but the common law action of account remains at a low level of development because of the fact that it was in practice superseded by the equitable jurisdiction of the Chancellor, who in the Bill for account had a more modern remedy operating under a more favourable and convenient procedure.

Covenant. This action is also an old one. Its writ directs *quod conventio teneatur.* The earliest use of the action is for the protection of the termor; at one time it is the lessee's only remedy. It early sends off a branch which is reckoned a real action because land is recovered,[1] in other cases the action results in money being obtained. It appears for a time as if covenant might be of general use wherever there is an agreement (*conventio*), might become, in fact, a general action for breach of contract; but the practice of the thirteenth century decides that there must be a sealed writing. A sacramental importance was attached to the use of the seal—*collatio sigilli*—and it was finally adopted as the only acceptable evidence of a covenant. Thus we come to the English formal contract, the Covenant under Seal. One curious limitation appears, and is maintained until the seventeenth century; Covenant cannot be brought for the recovery of a debt, though attested under seal. This action remains useful but in its own narrow sphere.

---

[1] This action of Covenant Real was abolished in 1833. See below, p. 62.

LECTURE VI

Trespass.[1] All the other personal actions branch out from one, namely Trespass. *Trespass* appears *circ.* 1250 as a means of charging a defendant with violence but no felony. The writ, as we have seen, contains the words *vi et armis contra pacem*, the procedure is enforced by a threat of outlawry, imprisonment is resorted to by way of mesne process, and the vanquished defendant is punished for his offence. He is not merely *in misericordia*, he is liable to a *capias pro fine*. There is a trifurcation, the writ varying according as the violence is done (1) to land, (2) to the body, or (3) to chattels. Speaking of trespass to land let us once more remember how trespass *quare clausum fregit* sends out the action for ejectment as a branch.

Trespass to the body (assaults and batteries) covered the whole ground of personal injury, and no great development was possible here. Trespass to goods, trespass *de bonis asportatis* is an action which results in damages, never return of the goods, for carrying goods off from the plaintiff's possession—and therefore the bailee can bring it.[2]

I have already said that the writ-making power wielded by the king and his chancellor was gradually curbed by our parliamentary constitution, and in Edward I's day it has become necessary to tell the Chancery that it is not to be too pedantic, but may make variations in the old formulas when a new case falls under an old rule. Some use was made of this liberty, but slowly and cautiously; it had not been intended that the chancellor should legislate. Thus we find one new writ of entry devised which is distinctly ascribed to the freedom of action left to the Chancery by the Statute of Westminster II, c. 24—it is the writ of entry *in consimili casu*.[3] But the most important use made of this liberty consisted in some extensions of the action of trespass. Gradually during Edward III's reign we find a few writs occurring which in form are

---

[1] See also above, pp. 38–40 and 43–50.

[2] On this subject see Holmes, *The Common Law, sub. tit.* Possession and Bailment.

[3] The writ of entry called *ad communem legem* lay where the flaw in the tenant's title originated in an alienation by a doweress or by a tenant by the curtesy, or for life or in tail, in excess of her or his powers (e.g. in fee) and lay only where the doweress, etc., was dead. The Statute of Gloucester c. 7 gave the remainderman an action by writ of entry, called *in casu proviso*, during the life of the alienor but only in case of alienation by a doweress. After the Statute of Westminster II the writ of entry *in consimili casu* was given during the life of the alienor to the remainderman in the other cases (F.N.B. 205, 206, 207).

extremely like writs of trespass—and they are actually called writs of trespass—but the wrong complained of does not always consist of a direct application of unlawful physical force to the body, lands, or goods of the plaintiff; sometimes the words *vi et armis* do not appear. Sometimes there is no mention of the king's peace. Still they are spoken of as writs of trespass, they appear in the Chancery Register as writs of trespass, mixed up with the writs which charge the defendant with violent assaults and asportations. The plaintiff is said to bring an action upon his case, or upon the special case, and gradually it becomes apparent that really a new and a very elastic form of action has thus been created. I think that lawyers were becoming conscious of this about the end of the fourteenth century. Certain procedural differences have made their appearance—when there is *vi et armis* in the writ, then the defendant if he will not appear may be taken by *capias ad respondendum* or may be outlawed—this cannot be if there is no talk of force and arms or the king's peace. Thus Case falls apart from Trespass—during the fifteenth century the line between them becomes always better marked. In 1503 (19 Hen. VII, c. 9) a statute takes note of the distinction; the process of *capias* is given in 'actions upon the case'. Under Henry VIII Fitzherbert in his *Abridgment* and his *Natura Brevium* treats of the 'Action sur la Case' as something different from the action of trespass—each has its precedents. The title of Case covers very miscellaneous wrongs—specially we may notice slander and libel (for which, however, there are but few precedents during the Middle Ages, since bad words are dealt with by the local courts, and defamation by the ecclesiastical courts), also damage caused by negligence, also deceit.

Case becomes a sort of general residuary action; much, particularly, of the modern law of negligence developed within it. Sometimes it is difficult to mark off case from trespass. The importance of the somewhat shadowy line between them was originally due to the fact that where *vis* and *arma* were not alleged there was no imprisonment in mesne process, nor was the defeated defendant liable to the judgment *quod capiatur pro fine*.

The judgment *quod capiatur pro fine* was abolished, formally, in 1694 (5 and 6 W. and M. c. 12), but had long before this been a mere form. The act recited that 'whereas in actions of trespass, ejectment, assault, and false imprisonment upon judgment entered against the defendant the courts do (*ex officio*) issue out process against such defendant for a fine to the Crown, for a breach of the peace thereby committed, which is not ascertained, but is usually compounded for a small sum by some officer of the court, but never estreated into the Exchequer, which officers do very often outlaw the defendants for the same to their very great damage', and the act proceeded to prohibit the issue of the writ of *capias pro fine* and to substitute a fixed payment of 6*s.* 8*d.* to be paid in the first place by the plaintiff on signing judgment but to be recovered by him as costs from the defendant.

Greater uniformity was introduced, partly by statute and partly by fiction, but still the distinction had to be observed. The plaintiff must sue either in case or in trespass, and upon the accuracy of his claim depended the success of his action. The well-known case of *Scott* v. *Shepherd* (2 W. Bl. 892 and 1 Sm. L.C.) turns upon this distinction, and is worth reading as illustrating the narrowness of the margin between the two. Even as late as 1890 parties in a case of wounding by a glancing shot fired from the defendant's gun are still arguing as to the appropriateness of trespass or case, the plaintiff contending, though without success, that in trespass negligence is immaterial and the defendant is liable for inevitable accident.[1] In 1875 Lord Bramwell (then Bramwell B.), in the case of *Holmes* v. *Mather*,[2] had explained the distinction thus: 'If the act that does the injury is an act of direct force, *vi et armis*, trespass is the proper remedy (if there is any remedy), where the act is wrongful either as being wilful or as being the result of negligence. Where the act is not wrongful for either of these reasons no action is maintainable, though trespass would be the proper form of action if it were wrongful.'

Sub-forms of Case become marked off, e.g. Case for negligence, for deceit, for words (slander and libel); but two great branches were thrown out which gain an independent life, and are generally important, viz. Assumpsit and Trover.

Assumpsit. The most curious offshoot of Case is Assumpsit and the great interest of this action lies in the fact that it becomes the general form by which contracts not under seal can be enforced by way of action for damages. Under the old law the contracts are formal, or 'real', the form required being the instrument under seal, the bond or covenant, and the 'real' contracts—the word 'real' being used in the sense of general jurisprudence—are protected by Debt-Detinue without it being seen that contract is the basis. Gradually however within the delictual action of Case various precedents collect in which the allegation is made that the defendant had undertaken to do something and then hurt the plaintiff either in his person or in his goods by doing it badly—by misfeasance.

---

[1] *Stanley* v. *Powell*, 1891, 1 Q.B. 86.   [2] L.R. 10 Ex. 261.

Further an important element in this progress is the idea of breach of contract as being deceit—the plaintiff suffers detriment by relying on the promise of the defendant. This point is brought out by Ames in the *Harvard Law Review*[1] in two masterly articles which should be read at length.

The having undertaken (*assumpsit*) to do something, makes its appearance as part of the cause of action in various writs upon the case. Thus we find an early group of cases, from Edward III's reign, in which the plaintiff seeks to recover compensation for some damage done to his person or goods by the active misconduct of the defendant, but still the defendant cannot be charged with a breach of the peace, as the plaintiff has put his person or his goods into the defendant's care. The defendant, for example, is a surgeon, and has unskilfully treated the plaintiff or his animals so that he or they have suffered some physical harm. In such cases we find an assumpsit alleged. It is necessary to allege that the defendant undertook the cure—had it not been so, according to the notions of the time, it might well have been urged that the harm was occasioned by the plaintiff's own folly in going to an inexpert doctor. A little later, in the fifteenth century, we have actions against bailees for negligence in the custody of goods intrusted to them, and here also it was necessary to allege an assumpsit. Again, there is another class of cases in which an undertaking is alleged—a seller has sold goods warranting them sound, and they have turned out unsound; the cause of action is regarded not as breach of contract, but as deceit. Thus in divers directions the law was finding materials for a generalisation, namely, that breach of an undertaking, an assumpsit, for which there was valuable consideration was a cause of action.

Gradually the line between mis-feasance and non-feasance was transcended, and gradually lawyers awoke to the fact that by extending an action of tort they had in effect created a new action by which parol contracts could be enforced. It is, I think, about the beginning of the sixteenth century that they begin to regard Assumpsit as a different form from Case, a form with precedents of its own and rules of its own. Then begins a new struggle to make Assumpsit do the work of Debt. Plaintiffs wish for this result because they desire to avoid that wager of law which is allowed in Debt, and defendants may fairly argue that according to the law of the land they are entitled to this ancient mode of proof. Professor Ames's article gives the stages of this struggle. Through the sixteenth century, an actual express agreement alone gives rise to Assumpsit, and therefore if Assumpsit is to be used to enforce a debt,

[1] 2 *H.L.R.* pp. 1 and 53.

for example for the price of goods sold and delivered, a new promise—a promise to pay that debt—must be alleged and proved. However, in 1602, *Slade's case* (4 Rep. 92 b) decides that Assumpsit may be brought where Debt would lie, and thenceforth Assumpsit supplants Debt as a means for recovering liquidated sums. In that case such a new promise had been alleged and the jury by a special verdict had found the bargain and sale to be proved but that 'there was no promise or taking upon him, besides the bargain aforesaid.'[1] Upon this finding the case was argued in the King's Bench and the action in Assumpsit was held to lie, the Court resolving that 'Every contract executory imports in itself an *assumpsit*, for when one agrees to pay money or to deliver anything, thereby he assumes or promises to pay or deliver it.'[2] Thenceforth the proof of the new promise becomes unnecessary. This form of Assumpsit takes the name of Indebitatus Assumpsit.

Some seven years later we have this action extended from cases of express executory contract to cases where the original bargain was an implied contract, in the sense that a contract is really to be implied from the facts of the case, for example, cases of actions for *Quantum meruit*.

Lastly, at some date between 1673 and 1705, Indebitatus Assumpsit is extended to actions upon Quasi-Contracts in which the element of contract is purely fictitious.

As we have already seen, this action of Assumpsit, which at least seems to us as of delictual origin, becomes the general mode of enforcing contracts even when a sum certain has to be recovered, and thus Assumpsit becomes a rival to and a substitute for Debt in which latter action the defendant may still wage his law. For some reason Debt was brought as late as 1824 in the case of *King* v.*Williams*, 2 B. and C. 538, when the defendant, although the court refused to assist him even to the extent of telling him how many helpers he needed, produced eleven helpers (*jurare decima manu*) and the plaintiff withdrew. Wager of law was, however, not formally abolished until 1833.[3]

Trover. One other great branch is thrown out by Case, namely Trover. For the history of this action see Ames's articles in the *Harvard Law Review*.[4] This also is an action for damages based upon a fictitious loss and finding and a subsequent conversion to the use of the defendant. Here there is no trespass, the defendant may be a perfectly innocent purchaser from the original wrongdoer; and there is no 'recuperation' —the gist of the action is the conversion.

---

[1] Rep. IV. 92 a.
[3] 3 and 4 Will. IV, c. 42, sec. 13.
[2] Rep. IV. at p. 94 a.
[4] 11 *H.L.R.* pp. 277 and 374.

I believe that Trover begins to appear about the middle of the sixteenth century. Gradually it begins to supplant Detinue, in which there is wager of law, and it becomes the normal mode of trying the title to moveable goods. The plaintiff charges that he was possessed of goods, that he lost them, that the defendant found them and converted them to his use. The court will not permit the defendant to dispute the loss and finding, but obliges him to answer the charge of conversion.

Since the provisions of sec. 78 of the Common Law Procedure Act of 1854, the old option, between paying the value of the chattel and restoring it to the successful plaintiff, is not necessarily left to the defendant, the court may order the restitution of the chattel. This statute has removed the original basis for the use of the terms by which we call lands 'real' and chattels 'personal' property; but the terms were adopted long ago and are likely to endure. The yet abiding distinction between lands and chattels lies in the two systems of intestate succession applicable to them.

Thus, by the beginning of the eighteenth century, Trespass and the various branches that it had thrown out had come to be the only forms of action that were in very common use. Trespass in ejectment, or ejectment, served the purpose of most of the real actions, though, as already said, there were occasions on which the latter had to be used. Assumpsit covered the old province of Debt, and a much larger province as well. Trover covered, and more than covered, the old province of Detinue. Trespass *vi et armis* still served for all cases in which the defendant had been guilty of directly applying unlawful force to the plaintiff's body, goods or chattels. Case covered the miscellaneous mass of other torts. Of the old actions Replevin maintained itself as the proper action against a distrainor. Covenant remained in use for the enforcement of promises under seal. The province of Account was gradually annexed by the Court of Chancery, and brought within the sphere of its equitable jurisdiction; and the use of the common law writs of dower, too, was to a great extent superseded by the relief given to the doweress in Courts of Equity, where new and valuable rights were given to her and to her personal representatives against the heir and his representatives which could not have been enforced by any process of the common law.[1] After 1833, when wager of law was abolished, Debt and Detinue were occasionally brought; but there was no longer much need for them, their place having been well filled by Assumpsit and Trover.

[1] See, for example, *Bamford* v. *Bamford*, 5 Hare 203, and *Williams* v. *Thomas*, 1909, 1 Ch. 713, by Cozens-Hardy, M.R., at p. 720.

LECTURE VII

Before parting with the forms of action a little should be said about attempts to classify them. Let me first remind you of a few sentences of Justinian's Institutes which have had a very important effect; *omnium actionum . . . summa divisio in duo genera deducitur: aut enim in rem sunt aut in personam*, Lib. IV. 6. § 1.[1] In a later chapter Justinian recognises a class of actions which are mixed, i.e. partly real, partly personal, IV. 6. 20.

Then there is another and a cross division of actions, some are *rei persequendae causa comparatae*, others are *poenae consequendae causa comparatae*, others belong to both these classes, IV. 6. 16.

Along with this we must take the classification of the obligations which are enforced by *actiones in personam*, III. 13; these are *ex contractu aut quasi ex contractu, ex maleficio aut quasi ex maleficio*.

Now these famous distinctions have at various times attracted English lawyers, and attempts were made to impose them upon the English materials, attempts which have never been very successful. Such phrases as criminal and civil, real and personal, possessory and proprietary, contractual and delictual are apparent already in Glanvill and prominent in Bracton's work, who makes use of them on the whole with great intelligence. These divisions of actions never, however, well fit the native stuff; they always cut across the form of the writs. A good example of this difficulty is seen in Trespass. It comes of penal stock, the defendant is liable to imprisonment, in the Middle Ages it covers all crimes short of felony—yet it is the ordinary civil action to recover damages for stepping on the land of another. Again, as we have seen, we have the writs of Entry standing between the indubitably proprietary and the indubitably possessory actions—this distinction is long regarded in England as a matter of degree, some writs are more 'in the right' than others.

[1] 'The leading division of all actions whatsoever, whether tried before a judge or a referee, is into two kinds, real and personal; that is to say the defendant is either under a contractual or delictual obligation to the plaintiff in which case the action is personal, and the plaintiff's contention is that the defendant ought to convey something to, or do something for him, or of a similar nature; or else, though there is no legal obligation between the parties, the plaintiff asserts a ground of action against someone else relating to some thing, in which case the action is real. Thus a man may be in possession of some corporeal thing, in which Titius claims a right of property and which the possessor affirms belongs to him; here if Titius sues for its recovery the action is real' (Moyle, II, 176, translating Institutes IV. 6. 1).

Bracton says, however, that there is no action *in rem* for moveable goods (fo. 102 *b*)—'At first sight it may appear that the action should be both real as well as personal, *tam in rem quam in personam*, since a particular thing is claimed, and the possessor is bound to give it up, but in truth it will be merely *in personam*, for he from whom the thing is claimed is not absolutely bound to restore the thing, but is bound in the disjunctive to restore the thing or its price, and by merely paying he is discharged, whether the thing be forthcoming or no. And therefore any one who claims a moveable for whatever cause, be it as having been carried off, or has having been lent, is bound to state its price, and count thus "I demand that such an one restore to me such a thing, of such a price", or "I complain that such an one detains from me, or has unjustly robbed me of such a thing of such a price", and if the price be not named the *vindicatio* of a moveable thing is bad.' The chattels of the middle ages were, I take it, both of a perishable kind and of a kind the value of which could be easily appraised; if the plaintiff got the *precium* of his ox he got what would do as well as his ox. However, this remark which made the reality or personality of the action depend not on the nature of the right asserted by the plaintiff but on the result of the judgment, has had results which as I think are much to be regretted. In the first place it is the origin of all our talk about real and personal property. The opinion comes to prevail that the action is 'real' if a favourable judgment gives possession of lands, tenements and hereditaments, 'personal' if damages are awarded and 'mixed' if both lands and damages are recovered. Gradually the terms 'things real' and 'things personal' begin to make their appearance and to supplant the old, and surely far better terms *terrae et tenementa* on the one hand, *bona et catalla* on the other. The law of intestate succession is in time made the test of realness and personalness; we are deprived of the legitimate use of a valuable pair of terms, because they have been put to an illegitimate use, and we have to talk about a term of years as a chattel real, but personal property. That is not all—having said that every action in which a chattel or its value is claimed is personal, are we not compelled to say that every such action is either founded on contract or founded on tort? Yes, that conclusion has been drawn, it is expressly drawn by Blackstone. The result of this has been to extend our notion of tort far beyond the Roman notion of *maleficium*. A chattel is stolen from me, and you in good faith buy it from the thief. I demand it from you, you require that I should prove my title in an action; my action is personal, and since it obviously is not founded on contract, it must be founded on tort.

What is the tort? I think we are obliged to say that the mere possessing of a moveable thing by one who is not entitled to possess it is a tort done to the true owner. It would surely have been far more convenient if we could have said that the owner's action is *in rem*, that he relies merely on the right of ownership, and does not complain that the possessor, who came by the thing quite honestly, has all along been doing him a wrong. The foundation for all this was abolished by the Common Law Procedure Act of 1854 which enabled a judge to order execution to issue for the return of a chattel detained without giving the defendant the option of paying the value assessed. (The effect of that section is now represented in the existing rules of court.) But I think we must still say that an action whereby an owner claims his chattel is an action founded on tort.

The attempt to distribute our personal forms under the two heads of contract and tort was never very successful or very important. In late days it was usual to put under the heading of Contract the following: Debt Covenant, Account, and Assumpsit; under the head of Tort— Trespass, Trover, Case, Replevin. Some writers put Detinue on one side of the line and some on the other. The truth was that (1) in substance Detinue might be an action founded on a contract or might be an action *ex maleficio*, or again might be an action founded on proprietary right which it would have been well could we have called real, while (2) in form Detinue was almost indistinguishable from Debt and both were closely allied to the writ of right; the law of the twelfth century to which these forms referred us saw little distinction between 'Give me up that piece of land for it is mine', 'Give me up that ox for it is mine', 'Give me up those £10 which are mine because I lent them to you'. In each case the claimant demands (*petit*) what is or ought to be his—the distinction between 'is' and 'ought to be' being hardly discerned. In very old cases we find a creditor called a demandant not a plaintiff, he is *petens* not *querens*. We have no longer to classify the forms, for they are gone; but I think that we still are obliged to say that every action for a chattel is founded on tort if it be not founded on contract, and thus to make our conception of tort considerably wider than our neighbour's notion of a delict.

Then as to land there have been difficulties. We have already noticed how Bracton says that there is no *actio in rem* for moveable goods. But he knew too much about Roman law to say that an action is *in rem* merely because the result of it is that the claimant will thereby obtain possession of land. Thus he says that the Novel Disseisin is a personal action founded on tort, it is *in personam* though the judgment will restore the plaintiff to the land. The plaintiff is not relying on a real right, but is merely complaining of a tort. His test of the 'reality' of an action is much rather the mesne than the final process. By mesne process is meant the procedure against a contumacious defendant for compelling him to plead. If the mesne process is merely against the person, by attacking him or seizing his body, then the action is *in personam*. If the procedure is against the thing in dispute the action is *in rem*. In the Novel Disseisin you proceed against the person; in a writ of right you proceed against the thing—the land is seized into the king's hand, and if the defendant, or rather tenant, remains contumacious, it is adjudged to the demandant. Gradually, however, as the influence of Roman law becomes weaker a different test is adopted, an action is real if it gives the person the very thing that he wants. Now the action of ejectment did this from Henry VII's day onwards but it did not receive the name of a real action, or of a mixed action for a very long while—it had been developed out of a purely personal action, the action for trespass, and if you will look at Blackstone's definitions you will see that they are carefully framed so as to keep ejectment out of the 'real' class.[1] I am not certain that it ever became correct to speak of ejectment as either real or mixed until the statute of 1833 abolished all real and mixed actions 'except' ejectment and some others, thus speaking as though ejectment were either real or mixed. The truth is that this classification never fitted our law very well. One of the actions abolished in 1833 as 'real or mixed' was an action of covenant real, i.e. an action founded on a covenant to convey or let land—an action in which a plaintiff could obtain judgment for the land, a judgment not for damages but *quod conventio teneatur*. To call an action based on covenant, or contractual right, a real or mixed action must of course seem very strange to students of 'general jurisprudence'; but it was the logical result of making the distinction turn on the answer to the question whether the plaintiff demands land or damages or both.

I do not see why at the present day under the Judicature Act an action for the recovery of land wherein the plaintiff relies merely on his proprietary right should not be called 'real'; but historically it is doubtless the representative of the action of ejectment and I see no reason for trying to reintroduce a distinction which has never fitted our law very well. The abiding influence of the history of ejectment is, I think, this, that if I am possessing land which you have a better right to possess I am incurring a liability to you for damages. You will read

[1] *Comm.* III, 117.

in Blackstone (III, 205) of the action for mesne profits. By means of piling fiction on fiction our courts came to the doctrine that when a plaintiff had recovered the land in an action of ejectment he could then proceed to treat the defendant's possession as one long continued trespass, and sue him in an action for mesne profits in which he could recover not only compensation for any damage done to the land, but compensation for loss of enjoyment. This doctrine still holds good, though its fictitious supports have been kicked away, and though nowadays one can get the land and the damages in one and the same action. But the result is that, however honest the wrongful possessor may be and however plausible may be the title under which he is possessing, he is doing a continuous wrong to him who has a better right to be in possession and will have to pay damages for it. Some modern judges have regretted the severity of our law against *bona fide* possessors holding under faulty titles, but it is the natural and abiding result of the disuse and abolition of the old real actions.

On the whole the lesson of this part of our legal history should be that it is dangerous to play with foreign terms unless we know very well what we are about.

It is worth while to consider for a moment why I am troubling you with these matters which might be called details of mere obsolete procedure. I must refer you again to Sir Henry Maine's good saying, 'Substantive law is secreted in the interstices of procedure.' So important in the past was this fact that the great textbooks take the form of treatises on procedure. Fitzherbert's book is called *De Natura Brevium*—and even at a much later date, indeed until quite recently, textbooks take the form of discussions as to when a man can bring this or that action—trespass, trover, detinue, or assumpsit. This dependence of right upon remedy it is that has given English law that close texture to which it owes its continuous existence despite the temptations of Romanism. As an illustration of the importance of this past history in forming the law of the present consider the question—why do we talk today of 'real' and 'personal' property? Any answer to this question must speak to us of obsolete forms of action.

And now to go back. We have seen a gradual process of formal decay which set in soon after the death of Edward I in 1307, and together with this formal decay a vigorous but contorted development of substantive law brought by fiction within the medieval forms. This is a long process; we may say that it even extends from 1307 to 1875. In this development there are two stages.

(1) The stage of evasory fiction, the last days of which are well described by Blackstone. During this stage a few relatively modern actions are made to do substantially all the duty of the courts—these actions are Trespass and its progeny. Again steps were dropped out of the procedure and merely replaced by the supposition that they had been taken. Thus the original writ was omitted, unless Error be brought upon the record, in which case, the record must be duly made up.

This stage is complicated by a process which slowly makes the courts of King's Bench and Exchequer competent courts for most practicable actions. The original distribution of jurisdiction between the courts was as follows. *Communia placita*—ordinary civil suits between subject and subject—belong to the Common Bench or Court of Common Pleas; *Placita coronae*, including, be it noticed, trespass *vi et armis*, to the King's Bench. The Court of Exchequer, as the financial court, has the duty of getting in the king's debts, but this includes getting in debts due to the king's debtor. The King's Bench and Exchequer have already therefore a footing in the field of civil actions and this footing they proceed to improve.

The King's Bench adopted the following fiction. Suppose for example that an action of debt is to be begun. First an action of trespass is begun and the defendant is arrested. He is thus in the custody of the marshal of the King's Bench and the court has jurisdiction in cases against its prisoners. Then follows a declaration in Debt by the plaintiff against this prisoner of the King's Bench.

The Exchequer fiction for the same purpose was known as a *quo minus*. The plaintiff pretends to be the king's debtor and alleges that he is being kept out of money due to him by the defendant whereby the less (*quo minus*) he is able to pay his debt to the king.

If we look for the motive which induced this stealing of business we may find it in the fact that the staff of the courts and to some extent the judges are paid by fees derived from the litigants. This result was also partly due to the fact that the serjeants had the exclusive right of audience in the court of Common Bench. The serjeants were created by royal writ—a man was appointed to the 'state and degree' of serjeant-at-law, an honour entailing, at least until the days of George III, an expensive banquet upon his creation. He became a member of the 'Order of the Coif'. Until the passing of the Judicature Act by custom all judges appointed must first be admitted serjeants-at-law, a custom which is believed to have had its origin in the terms of an Edwardian statute.[1] After the Judicature Act they disappeared. Now there were practitioners before the other courts, the Barristers (originally known as 'apprentices') who were interested in diverting business from the court in which serjeants alone had the right of audience to those in which they themselves could be heard. By such means our archaic procedure is being adapted to modern times but in an evasory and roundabout way by means of fictions.

(2) A new stage began in 1832 with the Unification of Process Act of that year.[2] So far no destruction of the forms of action was attempted, but the original and the mesne process are henceforward to be statutory and uniform in all personal actions.

In the following year the statute 3 and 4 Will. IV, c. 27, by sec. 36 abolished all the Real and Mixed actions excepting ejectment, *quare impedit* and the two writs of dower (the writ of right of dower and the writ of dower *unde nihil habet*): and in the same year the statute c. 42, sec. 13 made Debt and Detinue practicable and gave them a new lease of life by abolishing wager of law.

Still the forms of action remaining have to be kept apart and each must be used only within its proper precedents—trespass, case, assumpsit, trover, ejectment, debt and detinue.

The next great step was taken by the Common Law Procedure Act, 1852, sec. 3. Under this statute no form of action is to be mentioned in the writ, which is for the future to be a simple writ of summons. But even after this act the form of action remains of vital importance to the pleader for each action retains its own precedents, and although the choice of the proper form of action need no longer be made in the choice of writ it is merely deferred until the declaration.

The last great step comes with the Judicature Acts of 1873–5, the statutes effecting the fusion of equity and law. By these statutes and by the Rules of the Supreme Court made thereunder a new code of civil procedure was introduced, largely dependent for its working upon wide discretionary powers allowed to the judges. Henceforward not only is the writ a simple writ of summons but there are no longer any 'forms of action' in the old sense of the phrase.

The plaintiff is to state his case, not in any formula put into the king's

---

[1] 14 Edw. III. 16. Dealing only with Nisi Prius Commissions it says that one of the Commissioners must be either a judge of K.B. or C.P., Chief Baron of the Exchequer or a serjeant sworn. Under this a puisne Baron of the Exchequer would not be qualified unless he were a serjeant-at-law.

[2] 2 and 3 Will. IV, c. 33.

mouth but in his own (or his adviser's) words endorsed upon the writ, and his pleader is to say not upon what form of action he relies but merely what are the facts upon which he relies. Some differences there are in the procedure due to differences in the nature of the action, of the facts relied upon and of the rights to be enforced. Thus in some cases there is and in others there is not a right to a trial by jury, in some cases there is a right to special procedure for judgment by default if the claim is for a liquidated sum, and so forth. Much there is for practitioners to study in the Judicature Acts and the Rules of the Supreme Court, but it is no longer possible to regard any form of action as a separate thing.

This results in an important improvement in the statements of the law—for example in textbooks—for the attention is freed from the complexity of conflicting and overlapping systems of precedents and can be directed to the real problem of what are the rights between man and man, what is the substantive law.

SELECT WRITS

BEGINNING WITH THOSE RELATING TO LAND

Praecipe in Capite

Rex vicecomiti salutem. Praecipe X quod juste et sine dilatione reddat A unum mesuagium cum pertinentiis in Trumpingtone quod clamat esse jus et haereditatem suam et tenere de nobis in capite et unde queritur quod praedictus X ei injuste deforciat ut dicit. Et nisi fecerit, et praedictus A fecerit te securum de clamore suo prosequendo, tunc summone eum per bonos summonitores quod sit coram justiciariis nostris apud Westmonasterium[1] [tali die] ostensurus quare non fecerit. Et habeas ibi summonitores et hoc breve.[2]

The King to the sheriff greeting. Command X that justly and without delay he render to A one messuage with the appurtenances in Trumpington which he claims to be his right and inheritance, and to hold of us in chief and whereof he complains that the aforesaid X unjustly deforceth him. And unless he will do this, and (if) the aforesaid A shall give you security to prosecute his claim, then summon by good summoners the aforesd X that he be before our justices at Westminster [on such a day] to show wherefore he hath not done it. And have there the summoners and this writ.

Breve de recto

Rex K [a bishop, baron or other lord of manor] salutem. Praecipimus tibi quod sine dilatione plenum rectum teneas A de uno mesuagio cum pertinentiis in Trumpingtone quod clamat tenere de te per liberum servitium [unius denarii per annum] pro omni servitio, et quod X ei deforciat. Et nisi feceris, vicecomes de Cantabrigia faciat, ne amplius inde clamorem audiamus pro defectu recti.[3]

The King to K greeting. We command you that without delay you do full right to A of one messuage with the appurtenances in Trumpington which he claims to hold of you by free service of [so much] *per annum* for all service, of which X deforceth him. And unless you will do this, let the sheriff of Cambridge do it that we may hear no more clamour thereupon for want of right.

---

[1] I.e. In the court of Common Pleas.
[2] F.N.B. 51. Fitzherbert's *Natura Brevium* was published in 1534. (Fitzherbert ob. 1538.) When quoted F.N.B. without a date, the edition of 1553 is referred to. The translations added here and there for the assistance of the student are taken from the English edition of 1794, which preserved the paging of the edition of 1553.
[3] Bract. fo. 328a. F.N.B. 1 G.

Assisa Novae Disseisinae

Rex vicecomiti salutem. Questus est nobis A quod X injuste et sine judicio disseisivit eum de libero tenemento suo in Trumpingtone post [ultimum reditum domini regis de Brittannia in Angliam] (or other period of limitation). Et ideo tibi praecipimus quod, si praedictus A fecerit te securum de clamore suo prosequendo, tunc facias tenementum illud reseisiri de catallis quae in ipso capta fuerint et ipsum tenementum cum catallis esse in pace usque ad primam assisam cum justiciarii nostri ad partes illas venerint. Et interim facias xij liberos et legales homines de visneto illo videre tenementum illud et nomina illorum imbreviari. Et summoneas eos per bonos summonitores quod sint ad primam assisam coram prefatis justiciariis nostris, parati inde facere recognitionem. Et pone per vadium et salvos plegios praedictum X vel ballivum suum, si ipse inventus non fuerit, quod tunc sit ibi auditurus recognitionem illam. Et habeas ibi summonitorum nomina, plegios et hoc breve.[1]

The King to the sheriff greeting. A hath complained unto us that X unjustly and without judgment hath disseised him of his freehold in Trumpington after [the last return of our lord the king from Brittany into England]. And therefore we command you that, if the afores^d A shall make you secure to prosecute his claim, then cause that tenement to be reseised and[2] the chattels which were taken in it and the same tenement with the chattels to be in peace until the first assize when our justices shall come into those parts. And in the mean time you shall cause twelve free and lawful men of that venue to view that tenement and their names to be put into the writ. And summon them by good summoners that they be before the justices afores^d at the assize afores^d, ready to make recognizance thereupon. And put by gages and safe pledges the afores^d X or, if he shall not be found, his bailiff, that he be then there to hear that recognizance. And have there the (names of the) summoners, the pledges, and this writ.[3]

Assisa de Morte Antecessoris

Rex vicecomiti salutem. Si A fecerit te securum de clamore suo prosequendo tunc summoneas per bonos summonitores xij liberos et legales homines de visneto de Trumpingtone quod sint coram[4] justiciariis nostris ad primam assisam cum in partes illas venerint, parati sacramento recognoscere si B pater, [mater, frater, soror, avunculus, amita][5]

---

[1] Bract. fo. 179a. F.N.B. 1534, 69, where the wording has become slightly different.

[2] Quaere 'of'.   [3] F.N.B 177 E.

[4] It might be 'apud Westmonasterium' or *coram dilectis et fidelibus nostris* O. *et* P. (special commissioners).

[5] Beyond these 'degrees' writs of 'aiel' 'bezaiel' and 'cosinage' introduced by William Raleigh were used. For their forms see F.N.B. 220, 221.

praedicti A fuit seisitus in dominico suo ut de feodo de uno mesuagio cum pertinentiis in Trumpingtone die quo obiit, et si obiit post [period of limitation], et si idem A ejus haeres propinquior sit. Et interim praedictum mesuagium videant et nomina eorum inbreviari facias. Et summone per bonos summonitores X qui mesuagium praedictum tenet quod tunc sit ibi auditurus illam recognitionem. Et habeas ibi summonitores et hoc breve.[1]

The King to the sheriff greeting. If A shall make you secure, &c. then summon, &c. twelve free and lawful men of the neighbourhood of Trumpington that they be before our justices at the first assize when they shall come into those parts, ready to recognize by oath if B father [mother, brother, sister, uncle, aunt,] of the aforesᵈ A was seised in his demesne as of fee, of one messuage with the appurtenances in Trumpington the day whereon he died, and if he died after [the period of limitation] and if the same A be his next heir: and in the mean time let them view the sᵈ messuage, and cause their names to be put in the writ, and summon by good summoners X who now holds the aforesᵈ messuage, that he may be there to hear that recognizance; and have there the summoners and this writ.[2]

Brevia de Ingressu

Rex vicecomiti salutem. Praecipe X quod juste et sine dilatione reddat A unum mesuagium cum pertinentiis in Trumpingtone quod clamat esse jus et haereditatem suam et in quod praedictus X non habuit ingressum nisi—

a. per W qui illud ei dimisit qui inde injuste et sine judicio disseisivit eundem A [*or* B patrem ejusdem A cujus haeres ipse est] post [time of limitation].

b. per W cui V illud dimisit qui inde injuste etc., *as above.*

c. post disseisinam quam T inde injuste et sine judicio fecit B patri ejusdem A cujus haeres ipse est post [time of limitation] et unde queritur.

d. per K quondam virum ipsius A qui illud ei dimisit, cui ipsa in vita sua contradicere non potuit, ut dicit.

e. per W cui K quondam vir ipsius A qui illud ei dimisit, cui ipsa in vita sua contradicere non potuit, ut dicit.

f. post dimissionem quam K quondam vir ipsius A, cui ipsa in vita sua contradicere non potuit, inde fecit T ut dicit et unde queritur.

g. per W cui praedictus A illus dimisit dum non fuit compos mentis.

---

[1] Bracton, fo. 253 *b*.   [2] F.N.B. 195 E.

h. per W cui praedictus A illud dimisit dum fuit infra aetatem.

i. per W cui B pater praedicti A cujus haeres ipse est illud dimisit ad terminum qui praeteriit.

Et nisi fecerit summone eum per bonos summonitores quod sit coram justiciariis nostris apud Westmonasterium tali die ostensurus quare non fecerit. Et habeas ibi nomina summonitorum et hoc breve.

Note. The writs of entry given here are but a few out of great numbers of writs framed to cover almost every conceivable case of a flaw in the tenant's title. Amongst the writs recorded in Fitzherbert are (1) writs *super disseisinam*, or as they are sometimes called writs *de quibus*; where the flaw was a disseisin (of these *a*, *b* and *c* above are examples): (2) writs *ad communem legem, in casu proviso* and *in consimili casu* (explained above, p. 53 n.) where the flaw was an alienation in excess of powers by a doweress or a tenant by the curtesy, for life or in tail: (3) writs *cui in vita*, on alienation by a husband (examples *d*, *e* and *f* above) and (4) writs *cui ante divortium*, the same where the marriage has been dissolved (a strangely modern sound this has): (5) writs of *Dum non compos mentis* (example *g* above) and (6) of *Dum fuit infra aetatem* (example *h* above) on alienation by an idiot and an infant respectively: (7) writs of entry *ad terminum qui praeteriit* (example *i* above) where the flaw is the holding over of a lease: (8) writs of *intrusion*, where the flaw is similar to the wrong aimed at by the assize of Mort d'Ancestor and (9) the writ *sine assensu capituli* where the flaw is an alienation by an abbot &c. without his chapter's consent. Each of these writs may be in either of the three forms within the 'degrees' in the *per* (as *a*), in the *per* and *cui* (as *b*) and, outside the 'degrees', by virtue of the statute of Marlborough, in the *post* (as *c* in the above writs). Professor Maitland has in several instances omitted a few words for the sake of clearness.

Quare ejecit infra terminum[1]

Rex vicecomiti salutem. Si A fecerit te securum de clamore suo prosequendo tunc summoneas etc. X quod sit coram justiciariis etc. ostensurus quare deforciat praefato A unum mesuagium cum pertinentiis in Trumpingtone, quod M ei dimisit ad terminum qui nondum praeteriit, infra quem terminum idem M praefato X illud mesuagium vendidit, occasione cujus venditionis idem X praefatum A de mesuagio praedicto ejecit ut dicit. Et habeas ibi etc.

Trespass quare clausum fregit[2]

Rex vic. sal. Si A fecerit etc. tunc pone per vadium et salvos plegios X quod sit etc. ostensurus quare vi et armis clausum ipsius A apud

[1] F.N.B. 198 B. Fuit hoc breve inventum per discretum virum Will. de Merton. F.N.B. (1534 ed.), p. 81.

[2] This writ and the next one appear here without regard to their historical order for the purpose of showing in one group the greater writs relating to the land.

Trumpingtone fregit [et blada sua ibidem crescentia falcavit etc. etc.] et alia enormia ei intulit ad grave damnum ipsius A et contra pacem nostram. Et habeas ibi nomina plegiorum et hoc breve.

De ejectione firmae[1]

Rex vic. sal. Si A fecerit te securum etc. tunc pone etc. X quod sit coram etc. ostensurus quare vi et armis unum mesuagium apud Trumpingtone, quod M praefato A dimisit ad terminum qui nondum praeteriit, intravit et ipsum a firma sua praedicta ejecit et alia enormia ei intulit ad grave damnum ipsius A et contra pacem nostram. Et habeas ibi etc.

De Libertate Probanda

Rex vic. sal. Monstravit nobis A quod cum ipse liber homo sit et paratus libertatem suam probare, X clamans eum nativum suum vexat eum injuste. Et ideo tibi praecipimus quod si praedictus A fecerit te securum de libertate sua probanda, tunc ponas loquelam illam coram justiciariis nostris ad primam assisam cum in partes illas venerint quia hujusmodi probatio non pertinet ad te capienda. Et interim idem A pacem inde habere facias. Et dic praedicto X quod sit ibi loquelam suam versus praedictum A inde perfecturus si voluerit. Et habeas ibi hoc breve.

The King to the sheriff greeting. A hath showed unto us that whereas he is a free man and ready to prove his liberty, X claiming him to be his nief[2] unjustly vexes him; and therefore we command you, that if the aforesᵈ A shall make you secure touching the proving of his liberty, then put that plea before our justices at the first assizes, when they shall come into those parts, because proof of this kind belongeth not to you to take; and in the mean time cause the sᵈ A to have peace thereupon, and tell the aforesᵈ X that he may be there, if he will, to prosecute his plea thereof against the aforesᵈ A. And have there this writ.[3]

Debt, Detinue and Account

Rex vic. sal. Praecipe X quod juste et sine dilatione reddat A:

(*Breve de Debito*)[4]	centum libras quas ei debet et injuste detinet
(*Breve de Catallis reddendis*)[5]	catalla ad valentiam centum librarum quae ei injuste detinet
(*Breve de Compoto*)[6]	rationabile compotum suum de tempore quo fuit ballivus suus in Trumpingtone et receptorum denariorum ipsius A

---

[1] For a translation of the writ of ejectment see below, p. 73.
[2] nief (nativus) = villein.   [3] F.N.B. 77 F.
[4] F.N.B. 119 L.   [5] F.N.B. (1534 ed.), 40.   [6] F.N.B. 117 E.

ut dicit. Et nisi fecerit et praedictus A fecerit te securum de clamore suo prosequendo, tunc summone eum per bonos summonitores quod sit coram justiciariis nostris apud Westmonasterium [tali die] ostensurus quare non fecerit. Et habeas ibi summonitores et hoc breve.[1]

Covenant

Rex vic. sal. Praecipe X quod juste et sine dilatione teneat A conventionem factam inter ipsum A et [S patrem praedicti] X [cujus haeres ipse est,] de [uno messuagio]

et nisi fecerit &c. tunc summone &c.[2]

Trespass vi et armis[3]

Rex vic. sal. Si A fecerit te securum de clamore suo prosequendo tunc pone per vadium et salvos plegios X quod sit coram justiciariis nostris[4] &c. *tali die* ostensurus

(assault and battery)	quare vi et armis in ipsum A apud Trumpingtone insultum fecit et ipsum verberavit vulneravit et male tractavit, ita quod de vita ejus desperabatur
(false imprisonment)	quare vi et armis in ipsum A apud Trumpingtone insultum fecit et ipsum vulneravit imprisonavit et male tractavit
(trespass to land)	quare vi et armis clausum ipsius A apud Trumpingtone fregit.
(trespass to chattels)	quare vi et armis lapidem molarem[5] ipsius A precii xl. s. apud Trumpingtone fregit et bona et catalla sua precii tanti cepit et asportavit.
(ejectment)	quare vi et armis unum mesuagium apud Trumpingtone quod M praefato A dimisit ad terminum qui nondum praeteriit intravit et ipsum A a firma sua praedicta ejecit

---

[1] Note that these writs are in the same terms as the writ of Praecipe in Capite except for the words stating what the defendant is to deliver up to the demandant.

[2] F.N.B. (1534), 66, the ending is as for debt.

[3] F.N.B. 85–8. As an example we give the translation of the writ of Ejectment from Fitzherbert (1794 ed.). Several trespasses may be alleged in one writ.

[4] Or 'coram nobis tali die ubicumque fuerimus tunc in Angliae' if the writ be in the King's Bench.

[5] A mill stone.

et alia enormia ei intulit ad grave damnum ipsius A et contra pacem
nostram. Et habeas ibi nomina plegiorum et hoc breve.

The writ of Ejectment

The King to the sheriff greeting. If A shall make you secure &c. Then put by
gages and safe pledges X that he be before our justices at Westminster on
(such a day)[1] to show wherefore with force and arms he entered into one
messuage in Trumpington which M demised to the said A for a term which is
not yet passed and ejected him, the said A, from his farm aforesaid; and other
enormous things did, to the great damage of him the said A and against our
peace: and have there the names of the pledges and this writ. (F.N.B. 220 G.)

Trespass on the Case or Case

Rex vic. sal. &c. *as in Trespass* ostensurus:

quare[2] [here set out the matter complained of e.g.:—] in aqua de
Plim, per quam inter Humber et Gaunt navium et batellorum
communis est transitus, ex transverso aquae pilos defixit, per quod
quaedam navis cum triginta quarteriis brasii ipsius A submersa fuit,
et viginti quarteria brasii precii centum s. deperierunt. Et alia
enormia &c. *as in Trespass.*

The King to the sheriff &c. *as in Trespass* to show:
wherefore (e.g.:—) he fixed piles across the water of Plim along which,
between the Humber and Gaunt, there is a common passage for ships and boats,
whereby a certain ship, with thirty quarters of malt of him the s^d A, was sunk
under water, and twenty quarters of the malt of the price of one hundred
shillings perished; and other wrongs &c. *as in Trespass.*

Trespass on the Case in Assumpsit

Rex vic. sal. &c. *as in Trespass* ostensurus:

quare[3] [e.g.: for misfeasance] cum idem X ad dextrum oculum
ipsius A casualiter laesum bene et competenter curandum apud
Trumpingtone pro quadam pecuniae summa prae manibus soluta
assumpsisset, idem X curam suam circa oculum praedictum tam
negligenter et improvide apposuit, quod idem A defectu ipsius X
visum oculi praedicti totaliter amisit, ad damnum ipsius A viginti
librarum ut dicit. Et habeas ibi &c.

quare[3] [e.g.: for non-feasance] cum idem X tres currus pro victua-
libus ipsius A ad partes transmarinas ducendis pro certa pecuniae

---

[1] Thus for an action in the Common Pleas, but it would read 'that he be
before us on (such a day) wheresoever we shall then be in England' if it were
for an action in the King's Bench.

[2] F.N.B. 92 F.　　　[3] Blackstone, *Comm.* III, 122 note.　　　[4] F.N.B. 94 A.

summa prae manibus soluta infra certum terminum inter eos con-
cordatum facere et fabricare apud Trumpingtone assumpsisset, idem
X currus praedictos infra terminum praedictum facere et fabricare
non curavit per quod A diversa bona et catalla sua ad valentiam centum marcarum, quae in curribus praedictus duci debuissent, pro
defectu curruum praedictorum totaliter amisit ad grave damnum
ipsius A ut dicit et habeas &c.

The King to the sheriff greeting &c. *as in Trespass* to shew:
wherefore whereas he the s^d X undertook well and competently to cure the
right eye of the s^d A, which was accidentally injured, for a certain sum of money
beforehand received, he the same X so negligently and carelessly applied his
cure to the said eye, that the said A by the fault of him the said X totally lost
the sight of the said eye, to the damage of him the said A of twenty pounds, as he
saith, and have there &c.

wherefore whereas he the said X undertook to make and build three carriages
for conveying victuals of him the said A to parts beyond the sea for a certain
sum of money beforehand received, within a certain term between them agreed;
he the said X did not take care to make and build the carriages afores^d within
the term afores^d, by which he the s^d A hath wholly lost divers his goods and
chattels, to the value of one hundred marks, which ought to have been conveyed
in the carriages aforesaid, for want thereof to the great damage of him the said
A as it is said: and have there &c.

Case on Indebitatus Assumpsit[1]

The King to the sheriff &c. *as in Trespass* to shew:
for that, whereas the s^d X heretofore, to wit (*date and place*) was
indebted to the s^d A in the sum of —— for divers goods wares and
merchandises by the s^d A before that time sold and delivered to the
s^d X at his special instance and request.

and being so indebted, he the s^d X in consideration thereof
afterwards to wit (*date and place afores^d*) undertook and faithfully
promised the s^d A to pay him the s^d sum of money when he the
s^d X should be thereto afterwards requested.

Yet the s^d X, not regarding his said promise and undertaking but
contriving and fraudulently intending craftily and subtilly to
deceive and defraud the s^d A in this behalf, hath not yet paid the
s^d sum of money or any part thereof to the s^d A (although often-
times afterwards requested). But the s^d X to pay the same or any
part thereof hath hitherto wholly refused and still refuses, to the
damage of the s^d A of—pounds as it is said. And have you there &c.

---

[1] Stephen, *Pleading* (1824), p. 17.

Case for Trover[1]

The King to the sheriff greeting &c. *as in Trespass* to shew:

   for that, whereas the s^d A heretofore to wit [*date and place*] was lawfully possessed as of his own property, of certain goods and chattels to wit, twenty tables and twenty chairs of great value to wit of the value of — pounds of lawful money of great Britain;

     and, being so possessed thereof he the s^d A afterwards, to wit (*date and place afores*^d) casually lost the s^d goods and chattels out of his possession:

     and the same afterward, to wit (*date and place afores*^d) came into the possession of the s^d X by finding;

Yet the s^d X well knowing the s^d goods and chattels to be the property of the s^d A and of right to belong and appertain to him, but, contriving and fraudulently intending craftily and subtilly to deceive and defraud the s^d A in this behalf, hath not as yet delivered the s^d goods and chattels, or any part thereof, to the s^d A (although often requested so to do) but so to do hath hitherto wholly refused and still refuses; and afterwards to wit (*date and place afores*^d) converted and disposed of the s^d goods and chattels to his the s^d X's own use,

   to the damage of the s^d A of — pounds as it is said; and have you there &c.

---

[1] Stephen, *Pleading* (1824), p. 19.